Barlasch of the Guard

Henry Seton Merriman

BIBLIOLIFE

BARLASCH OF THE GUARD

HENRY SETON MERRIMAN

AUTHOR OF

"THE SOWERS," "THE ISLE OF UNREST," "THE VELVET GLOVE"
"THE VULTURES," ETC. ETC.

" And they that have not heard shall understand "

SMITH, ELDER & CO., 15, WATERLOO PLACE

1903

CONTENTS.

CONTENTS.

BARLASCH OF THE GUARD.

CHAPTER I.

ALL ON A SUMMER'S DAY.

Il faut devoir lever les yeux pour regarder ce qu'on aime.

A FEW children had congregated on the steps of the Marienkirche at Dantzig, because the door stood open. The verger, old Peter Koch—on week days a locksmith—had told them that nothing was going to happen; had been indiscreet enough to bid them go away. So they stayed, for they were little girls.

A wedding was in point of fact in progress within the towering walls of the Marienkirche—a cathedral built of red brick in the great days of the Hanseatic League.

"Who is it?" asked a stout fishwife, stepping over the threshold to whisper to Peter Koch.

B

"It is the younger daughter of Antoine Sebastian," replied the verger, indicating with a nod of his head the house on the left-hand side of the Frauengasse where Sebastian lived. There was a wealth of meaning in the nod. For Peter Koch lived round the corner in the Kleine Schmiedegasse, and of course—well, it is only neighbourly to take an interest in those who drink milk from the same cow and buy wood from the same Jew.

The fishwife looked thoughtfully down the Frauengasse where every house has a different gable, and none of less than three floors within the pitch of the roof. She singled out No. 36, which has a carved stone balustrade to its broad verandah and a railing of wrought-iron on either side of the steps descending from the verandah to the street.

"They teach dancing?" she inquired.

And Koch nodded again, taking snuff.

"And he—the father?"

"He scrapes a fiddle," replied the verger, examining the lady's basket of fish in a non-committing and final way. For a locksmith is almost as confidential an adviser as a notary. The Dantzigers, moreover, are a thrifty race and keep their money in a safe place; a habit which was to cost many of them their lives before the coming of another June.

The marriage service was a long one and not

exhilarating. Through the open door came no sound of organ or choir, but the deep and monotonous drawl of one voice. There had been no ringing of bells. The north countries, with the exception of Russia, require more than the ringing of bells or the waving of flags to warm their hearts. They celebrate their festivities with good meat and wine consumed decently behind closed doors.

Dantzig was in fact under a cloud. No larger than a man's hand, this cloud had risen in Corsica forty-three years earlier. It had overshadowed France. Its gloom had spread to Italy, Austria, Spain; had penetrated so far north as Sweden; was now hanging sullen over Dantzig, the greatest of the Hanseatic towns, the Free City. For a Dantziger had never needed to say that he was a Pole or a Prussian, a Swede or a subject of the Czar. He was a Dantziger. Which is tantamount to having for a postal address in these wordy days a single name that is marked on the map.

Napoleon had garrisoned the Free City with French troops some years earlier, to the sullen astonishment of the citizens. And Prussia had not objected for a very obvious reason. Within the last fourteen months the garrison had been greatly augmented. The clouds seemed to be gathering over this prosperous city of the north, where, however, men continued to eat and drink, to marry and to be given in marriage as in another city of the plain.

Peter Koch replaced his snuff-stained handkerchief in the pocket of his rusty cassock and stood aside. He murmured a few conventional words of blessing, hard on the heels of stronger exhortations to the waiting children. And Désirée Sebastian came out into the sunlight—Désirée Sebastian no more.

That she was destined for the sunlight was clearly written on her face and in her gay, kind blue eyes. She was tall and straight and slim, as are English and Polish and Danish girls, and none other in all the world. But the colouring of her face and hair was more pronounced than in the fairness of Anglo-Saxon youth. For her hair had a golden tinge in it, and her skin was of that startlingly milky whiteness which is only found in those who live round the frozen waters. Her eyes, too, were of a clearer blue —like the blue of a summer sky over the Baltic sea. The rosy colour was in her cheeks, her eyes were laughing. This was a bride who had no mis-givings.

On seeing such a happy face returning from the altar to-day the observer concludes that the bride has assuredly attained her desire; that she has secured a title; that the pre-nuptial settlement is safely signed and sealed.

But Désirée had none of these things. It was nearly a hundred years ago.

Her husband must have whispered some laughing comment on Koch, or another appeal to her quick sense of the humorous, for she looked into his changing face and gave a low, girlish laugh of amusement as they descended the steps together into the brilliant sunlight.

Charles Darragon wore one of the countless uniforms that enlivened the outward world in the great days of the greatest captain that history has seen. He was unmistakably French—unmistakably a French gentleman, as rare in 1812 as he is to-day. To judge from his small head and clean-cut features, fine and mobile; from his graceful carriage and slight limbs, this man was one of the many bearing names that begin with the fourth letter of the alphabet since the Terror only.

He was merely a lieutenant in a regiment of Alsatian recruits; but that went for nothing in the days of the Empire. Three kings in Europe had begun no farther up the ladder.

The Frauengasse is a short street, made narrow by the terrace that each house throws outward from its face, each seeking to gain a few inches on its neighbour. It runs from the Marienkirche to the Frauenthor, and remains to-day as it was built three hundred years ago.

Désirée nodded and laughed to the children, who interested her. She was quite simple and womanly, as some women, it is to be hoped, may succeed in continuing until the end of time. She was always pleased to see children; was glad, it seemed, that they should have congregated on the steps to watch her pass. Charles, with a faint and unconscious reflex of that grand manner which had brought his father to the guillotine, felt in his pocket for money, and found none.

He jerked his hand out with widespread fingers, in a gesture indicative of familiarity with the nakedness of the land.

"I have nothing, little citizens," he said with a mock gravity; "nothing but my blessing."

And he made a gay gesture with his left hand over their heads, not the act of benediction, but of peppering, which made them all laugh. The bride and bridegroom passing on joined in the laughter with hearts as light and voices scarcely less youthful.

The Frauengasse is intersected by the Pfaffengasse at right angles, through which narrow and straight street passes much of the traffic towards the Langenmarkt, the centre of the town. As the little bridal procession reached the corner of this street, it halted at the approach of some mounted troops.

There was nothing unusual in this sight in the streets of Dantzig, which were accustomed now to the clatter of the Saxon cavalry.

But at the sight of the first troopers Charles Darragon threw up his head with a little exclamation of surprise.

Désirée looked at him and then turned to follow the direction of his gaze.

"What are these?" she murmured. For the uniforms were new and unfamiliar.

"Cavalry of the Old Guard," replied her husband, and as he spoke he caught his breath.

The horsemen vanished into the continuation of the Pfaffengasse, and immediately behind them came a travelling carriage, swung on high wheels, three times the size of a Dantzig drosky, white with dust. It had small square windows. As Désirée drew back in obedience to a movement of her husband's arm, she saw a face for an instant—pale and set— with eyes that seemed to look at everything and yet at something beyond.

"Who was it? He looked at you, Charles," said Désirée.

"It is the Emperor," answered Darragon. His face was white. His eyes were dull, like the eyes of one who has seen a vision and is not yet back to earth.

Désirée turned to those behind her.

"It is the Emperor," she said, with an odd ring in her voice which none had ever heard before. Then she stood looking after the carriage.

Her father, who was at her elbow—tall, white-haired, with an aquiline, inscrutable face—stood in a like attitude, looking down the Pfaffengasse. His hand was raised before his face with outspread fingers which seemed rigid in that gesture, as if lifted hastily to screen his face and hide it.

"Did he see me?" he asked in a low voice which only Désirée heard.

She glanced at him, and her eyes, which were clear as a cloudless sky, were suddenly shadowed by a suspicion quick and poignant.

"He seemed to see everything, but he only looked at Charles," she answered. For a moment they all stood in the sunshine looking towards the Langenmarkt where the tower of the Rathhaus rose above the high roofs. The dust raised by the horses' feet and the carriage wheels slowly settled on their bridal clothes.

It was Désirée who at length made a movement to continue their way towards her father's house.

"Well," she said with a slight laugh, "he was not bidden to my wedding, but he has come all the same."

Others laughed as they followed her. For a bride at the church-door, or a judge on the bench, or a criminal on the scaffold-steps, need make but a very small joke to cause merriment. Laughter is often nothing but the froth of tears.

There were faces suddenly bleached in the little group of wedding-guests, and none were whiter than the handsome features of Mathilde Sebastian, Désirée's elder sister, who looked angry, had frowned at the children, and seemed to find this simple wedding too bourgeois for her taste. She carried her head with an air that told the world not to expect that she should ever be content to marry in such a humble style, and walk from the church in satin slippers like any daughter of a burgher.

This, at all events, was what old Koch the lock-smith must have read in her beautiful, discontented face.

"Ah! ah!" he muttered to the bolts as he shot them. "But it is not the lightest hearts that quit the church in a carriage."

So simple were the arrangements that bride and bridegroom and wedding-guests had to wait in the street while the servant unlocked the front door of No. 36 with a great key hurriedly extracted from her apron-pocket.

There was no unusual stir in the street. The

windows of one or two of the houses had been decorated with flowers. These were the houses of friends. Others were silent and still behind their lace curtains, where there doubtless lurked peeping and criticizing eyes—the house of a neighbour.

The wedding-guests were few in number. Only one of them had a distinguished air, and he, like the bridegroom, wore the uniform of France. He was a small man, somewhat brusque in attitude, as became a soldier of Italy and Egypt. But he had a pleasant smile and that affability of manner which many learnt in the first years of the great Republic. He and Mathilde Sebastian never looked at each other: either an understanding or a misunderstanding.

The host, Antoine Sebastian, played his part well enough when he remembered that he had a part to play. He listened with a kind attention to the story of a very old lady, who it seemed had been married herself, but it was so long ago that the human interest of it all was lost in a pottle of petty detail which was all she could recall. Before the story was half finished, Sebastian's attention had strayed elsewhere, though his spare figure remained in its attitude of attention and polite forbearance. His mind had, it would seem, a trick of thus wandering away and leaving his body rigid in the last attitude that it had dictated.

Sebastian did not notice that the door was open and all the guests were waiting for him to lead the way.

"Now, old dreamer," whispered Désirée, with a quick pinch on his arm, "take the Grafin upstairs to the drawing-room and give her wine. You are to drink our healths, remember."

"Is there wine?" he asked with a vague smile. "Where has it come from?"

"Like other good things, my father-in-law," replied Charles with his easy laugh, "it comes from France."

They spoke together thus in confidence, in the language of that same sunny land. But when Sebastian turned again to the old lady, still recalling the details of that other wedding, he addressed her in German, offering his arm with a sudden stiffness of gesture which he seemed to put on with the change of tongue.

They passed up the low time-worn steps arm-in-arm, and beneath the high carved doorway, whereon some pious Hanseatic merchant had inscribed his belief that if God be in the house there is no need of a watchman, emphasizing his creed by bolts and locks of enormous strength, and bars to every window.

The servant in her Samland Sunday dress, having

shaken her fist at the children, closed the door behind the last guest, and, so far as the Frauengasse was concerned, the exciting incident was over. From the open window came only the murmur of quiet voices, the clink of glasses at the drinking of a toast, or a laugh in the clear voice of the bride herself. For Désirée persisted in her optimistic view of these proceedings, though her husband scarcely helped her now at all, and seemed a different man since the passage through the Pfaffengasse of that dusty travelling carriage which had played the part of the stormy petrel from end to end of Europe.

CHAPTER II.

A CAMPAIGNER.

Not what I am, but what I Do, is my Kingdom.

DÉSIRÉE had made all her own wedding-clothes. "Her poor little marriage-basket," she called it. She had even made the cake which was now cut with some ceremony by her father.

"I tremble," she exclaimed aloud, "to think what it may be like in the middle."

And Mathilde was the only person there who did not smile at the unconscious admission. The cake was still under discussion, and the Gräfin had just admitted that it was almost as good as that other cake which had been consumed in the days of Frederick the Great, when the servant called Désirée from the room.

"It is a soldier," she said in a whisper at the head of the stairs. "He has a paper in his hand. I know what that means. He is quartered on us."

Désirée hurried downstairs. In the entrance-hall, a broad-built little man stood awaiting her. He was stout and red, with hair all ragged at the temples, almost white. His eyes were lost behind shaggy eyebrows. His face was made broader by little whiskers stopping short at the level of his ear. He had a snuff-blown complexion, and in the wrinkles of his face the dust of a dozen campaigns seemed to have accumulated.

"Barlasch," he said curtly, holding out a long strip of blue paper. "Of the Guard. Once a sergeant. Italy, Egypt, the Danube."

He frowned at Désirée while she read the paper in the dim light that filtered through the twisted bars of the fanlight above the door.

Then he turned to the servant who stood, comely and breathless, looking him up and down.

"Papa Barlasch," he added for her edification, and he drew down his left eyebrow with a jerk, so that it almost touched his cheek. His right eye, grey and piercing, returned her astonished gaze with a fierce steadfastness.

"Does this mean that you are quartered upon us?" asked Désirée without seeking to hide her disgust. She spoke in her own tongue.

"French?" said the soldier, looking at her. "Good. Yes. I am quartered here. Thirty-six, Frauengasse. Sebastian, musician. You are lucky to get me. I always give satisfaction—ha!"

He gave a curt laugh in one syllable only. His left arm was curved round a bundle of wood bound together by a red pocket-handkerchief not innocent of snuff. He held out this bundle to Désirée, as Solomon may have held out some great gift to the Queen of Sheba to smooth the first doubtful steps of friendship.

Désirée accepted the gift and stood in her wedding-dress holding the bundle of wood against her breast. Then a gleam of the one grey eye that was visible conveyed to her the fact that this walnut-faced warrior was smiling. She laughed gaily.

"It is well," said Barlasch. "We are friends. You are lucky to get me. You may not think so now. Would this woman like me to speak to her in Polish or German?"

"Do you speak so many languages?"

He shrugged his shoulders and spread out his arms as far as his many burdens allowed. For he was hung round with a hundred parcels and packages.

"The Old Guard," he said, "can always make itself understood."

He rubbed his hands together with the air of a brisk man ready for any sort of work.

"Now, where shall I sleep?" he asked. "One is not particular, you understand. A few minutes and one is at home—perhaps peeling the potatoes. It is only a civilian who is ashamed of using his knife on a potato. Papa Barlasch, they call me."

Without awaiting an invitation he went forward towards the kitchen. He seemed to know the house by instinct. His progress was accompanied by a clatter of utensils like that which heralds the coming of a carrier's cart.

At the kitchen door he stopped and sniffed loudly. There certainly was a slight odour of burning fat. Papa Barlasch turned and shook an admonitory finger at the servant, but he said nothing. He looked round at the highly polished utensils, at the table and floor both alike scrubbed clean by a vigorous northern arm. And he was kind enough to nod approval.

"On a campaign," he said to no one in particular, "a little bit of horse thrust into the cinders on the end of a bayonet—but in times of peace . . ."

He broke off and made a gesture towards the saucepans which indicated quite clearly that he was—between campaigns—inclined to good living.

"I am a rude fork," he jerked to Désirée over his shoulder in the dialect of the Côtes du Nord.

"How long will you be here?" asked Désirée, who was eminently practical. A billet was a misfortune which Charles Darragon had hitherto succeeded in warding off. He had some small influence as an officer of the head-quarters' staff.

Barlasch held up a reproving hand. The question, he seemed to think, was not quite delicate.

"I pay my own," he said. "Give and take—that is my motto. When you have nothing to give . . . offer a smile."

With a gesture he indicated the bundle of firewood which Désirée still absent-mindedly carried against her white dress. He turned and opened a cupboard low down on the floor at the left-hand side of the fireplace. He seemed to know by an instinct usually possessed by charwomen and other domesticated persons of experience where the firewood was kept. Lisa gave a little exclamation of surprise at his impertinence and his perspicacity. He took the firewood, unknotted his handkerchief, and threw his offering into the cupboard. Then he turned and perceived for the first time that Désirée had a bright ribbon at her waist and on her shoulders; that a thin chain of gold was round her throat and that there were flowers at her breast.

"A fête?" he inquired curtly.

"My marriage fête," she answered. "I was married half an hour ago."

He looked at her beneath his grizzled brows. His face was only capable of producing one expression—a shaggy weather-beaten fierceness. But, like a dog which can express more than many human beings, by a hundred instinctive gestures he could, it seemed,

C

dispense with words on occasion and get on quite as well without them. He clearly disapproved of Désirée's marriage, and drew her attention to the fact that she was no more than a schoolgirl with an inconsequent brain, and little limbs too slight to fight a successful battle in a world full of cruelty and danger.

Then he made a gesture half of apology as if recognizing that it was no business of his, and turned away thoughtfully.

"I had troubles of that sort myself," he explained, putting together the embers on the hearth with the point of a twisted, rusty bayonet, " but that was long ago. Well, I can drink your health all the same, mademoiselle."

He turned to Lisa with a friendly nod and put out his tongue, in the manner of the people, to indicate that his lips were dry.

Désirée had always been the housekeeper. It was to her that Lisa naturally turned in her extremity at the invasion of her kitchen by Papa Barlasch. And when that warrior had been supplied with beer it was with Désirée, in an agitated whisper in the great dark dining-room with its gloomy old pictures and heavy carving, that she took counsel as to where he should be quartered.

The object of their solicitude himself interrupted their hurried consultation by opening the door and putting his shaggy head round the corner of it.

"It is not worth while to consult long about it," he said. "There is a little room behind the kitchen, that opens into the yard. It is full of boxes. But we can move them—a little straw—and there!"

With a gesture he described a condition of domestic peace and comfort which far exceeded his humble requirements.

"The blackbeetles and I are old friends," he concluded cheerfully.

"There are no blackbeetles in the house, monsieur," said Désirée, hesitating to accept his proposal.

"Then I shall resign myself to my solitude," he answered. "It is quiet. I shall not hear the patron touching on his violin. It is that which occupies his leisure, is it not?"

"Yes," answered Désirée, still considering the question.

"I too am a musician," said Papa Barlasch, turning towards the kitchen again. "I played a drum at Marengo."

And as he led the way to the little room in the yard at the back of the kitchen, he expressed by a shake of the head a fellow-feeling for the gentleman upstairs, whose acquaintance he had not yet made, who occupied his leisure by touching the violin.

They stood together in the small apartment which

Barlasch, with the promptitude of an experienced con- queror, had set apart for his own accommodation.

"Those trunks," he observed casually, "were made in France"—a mental note which he happened to make aloud, as some do for better remembrance. "This solid girl and I will soon move them. And you, mademoiselle, go back to your wedding."

"The good God be merciful to you," he added under his breath when Désirée had gone.

She laughed as she mounted the stairs, a slim white figure amid the heavy woodwork long since blackened by time. The stairs made no sound beneath her light step. How many weary feet had climbed them since they were built! For the Dantzigers have been a people of sorrow, torn by wars, starved by siege, tossed from one conqueror to another from the beginning until now.

Désirée excused herself for her absence and frankly gave the cause. She was disposed to make light of the incident. It was natural to her to be optimistic. Both she and Mathilde made a practice of withholding from their father's knowledge the smaller worries of daily life which sour so many women and make them whine on platforms to be given the larger woes.

She was glad to note that her father did not attach much importance to the arrival of Papa Barlasch, though Mathilde found opportunity to convey her displeasure at the news by a movement of the eye-brows.

Antoine Sebastian had applied himself seriously now to his *rôle* of host, so rarely played in the Frauengasse. He was courteous and quick to see a want or a possible desire of any one of his guests. It was part of his sense of hospitality to dismiss all personal matters, and especially a personal trouble, from public attention.

"They will attend to him in the kitchen, no doubt," he said with that grand air which the dancing academy tried to imitate.

Charles hardly noted what Désirée said. So sunny a nature as his might have been expected to make light of a minor trouble, more especially the minor trouble of another. He was unusually thoughtful. Some event of the morning had, it would appear, given him pause on his primrose path. He glanced more than once over his shoulder towards the window, which stood open. He seemed at times to listen.

Suddenly he rose and went to the window. His action caused a brief silence, and all heard the clatter of a horse's feet and the quick rattle of a sword against spur and buckle.

After a glance he came back into the room.

"Excuse me," he said, with a bow towards Mathilde. "It is, I think, a messenger for me."

And he hurried downstairs. He did not return at
once, and soon the conversation became general again.

"You," said the Gräfin, touching Désirée's arm with
her fan, "you, who are now his wife, must be dying to
know what has called him away. Do not consider
the 'convenances,' my child."

Désirée, thus admonished, followed Charles. She
had not been aware of this consuming curiosity until
it was suggested to her.

She found Charles standing at the open door. He
thrust a letter into his pocket as she approached him,
and turned towards her the face that she had seen for
a moment when he drew her back at the corner of the
Pfaffengasse to allow the Emperor's carriage to pass on
its way. It was the white, half-stupefied face of one
who has for an instant seen a vision of things not
earthly.

"I have been sent for by the . . . I am wanted
at head-quarters," he said vaguely. "I shall not be
long . . ."

He took his shako, looked at her with an odd
attempt to simulate cheerfulness, kissed her fingers
and hurried out into the street.

CHAPTER III.

FATE.

We pass; the path that each man trod
Is dim; or will be dim, with weeds.

WHEN Désirée turned towards the stairs, she met the guests descending. They were taking their leave as they came down, hurriedly, like persons conscious of having outstayed their welcome.

Mathilde listened coldly to the conventional excuses. So few people recognize the simple fact that they need never apologize for going away. Sebastian stood at the head of the stairs bowing in his most Germanic manner. The urbane host, with a charm entirely French, who had dispensed a simple hospitality so easily and gracefully a few minutes earlier, seemed to have disappeared behind a pale and formal mask.

Désirée was glad to see them go. There was a sense of uneasiness, a vague unrest in the air. There was something amiss. The wedding-party had been a failure. All had gone well and merrily up to a certain point—at the corner of the Pfaffengasse, when the dusty travelling carriage passed across their path.

From that moment there had been a change. A shadow seemed to have fallen across the sunny nature of the proceedings; for never had bride and bridegroom set forth together with lighter hearts than those carried by Charles and Désirée Darragon down the steps of the Marienkirche.

During its progress across the whole width of Germany, the carriage had left unrest behind it. Men had travelled night and day to stand sleepless by the roadside and see it pass. Whole cities had been kept astir till morning by the mere rumour that its flying wheels would be heard in the streets before dawn. Hatred and adoration, fear and that dread tightening of the heartstrings which is caused by the shadow of the superhuman, had sprung into being at the mere sound of its approach.

When therefore it passed across the Frauengasse, throwing its dust upon Désirée's wedding-dress, it was only fulfilling a mission. When it broke in upon the lives of these few persons seeking dimly for their happiness—as the heathen grope for an unknown God —and threw down carefully constructed plans, swept aside the strongest will and crushed the stoutest heart, it was only working out its destiny. The dust sprinkled on Désirée's hair had fallen on the faces of thousands of dead. The unrest that entered into the quiet little house on the left-hand side of the

Frauengasse had made its way across a thousand thresholds, of Arab tent and imperial palace alike. The lives of millions were affected by it, the secret hopes of thousands were undermined by it. It disturbed the sleep of half the world, and made men old before their time.

"More troops must have arrived," said Désirée, already busying herself to set the house in order, "since they have been forced to billet this man with us. And now they have sent for Charles, though he is really on leave of absence."

She glanced at the clock.

"I hope he will not be late. The chaise is to come at four o'clock. There is still time for me to help you."

Mathilde made no answer. Their father stood near the window. He was looking out with thoughtful eyes. His face was drawn downwards by a hundred fine wrinkles. It was the face of one brooding over a sorrow or a vengeance. There was something in his whole being suggestive of a bygone prosperity. This was a lean man who had once been well-seeming.

"No!" said Désirée gaily, "we were a dull company. We need not disguise it. It all came from that man crossing our path in his dusty carriage."

"He is on his way to Russia," Sebastian said jerkily. "God spare me to see him return!"

Désirée and Mathilde exchanged a glance of uneasiness. It seemed that their father was subject to certain humours which they had reason to dread. Désirée left her occupation and went to him, linking her arm in his and standing beside him.

"Do not let us think of disagreeable things to-day," she said. "God will spare you much longer than that, you depressing old wedding-guest!"

He patted her hand which rested on his arm and looked down at her with eyes softened by affection. But her fair hair, rather tumbled, which met his glance must have awakened some memory that made his face a marble mask again.

"Yes," he said grimly, "but I am an old man and he is a young one. And I want to see him dead before I die."

"I will not have you think such bloodthirsty thoughts on my wedding-day," said Désirée. "See, there is Charles returning already, and he has not been absent ten minutes. He has some one with him— who is it? Papa . . . Mathilde, look! Who is it coming back with Charles in such a hurry?"

Mathilde, who was setting the room in order, glanced through the lace curtains.

"I do not know," she answered indifferently. "Just an ordinary man."

Désirée had turned away from the window as if to go downstairs and meet her husband. She paused and looked back again over her shoulder towards the street.

"Is it?" she said rather oddly. "I do not know —I——"

And she stood with the incompleted sentence on her lips waiting irresolutely for Charles to come upstairs.

In a moment he burst into the room with all his usual exuberance and high spirit.

"Picture to yourselves!" he cried, standing in the doorway with his arms extended before him. "I was hurrying to head-quarters when I ran into the embrace of my dear Louis—my cousin. I have told you a hundred times that he is brother and father and everything to me. I am so glad that he should come to-day of all days."

He turned towards the stairs with a gesture of welcome, still with his two arms outheld, as if inviting the man, who came rather slowly upstairs, to come to his embrace and to the embrace of those who were now his relations.

"There was a little suspicion of sadness—I do not know what it was—at the table; but now it is all gone. All is well now that this unexpected guest has come. This dear Louis."

He went to the landing as he spoke, and returned bringing by the arm a man taller than himself and darker, with a still brown face and steady eyes set close together. He had a lean look of good breeding.

"This dear Louis!" repeated Charles. "My only

relative in all the world.   My cousin, Louis d'Arragon. But he, *par exemple*, spells his name in two words."

The man bowed gravely—a comprehensive bow; but he looked at Désirée.

"This is my father-in-law," continued Charles breathlessly.   "Monsieur Antoine Sebastian, and Désirée and Mathilde—my wife, my dear Louis—your cousin, Désirée."

He had turned again to Louis and shook him by the shoulders in the fulness of his joy.   He had not distinguished between Mathilde and Désirée, and it was towards Mathilde that D'Arragon looked with a polite and rather formal repetition of his bow.

"It is I . . . I am Désirée," said the younger sister, coming forward with a slow gesture of shyness.

D'Arragon took her hand.

"I have been happy," he said, "in the moment of my arrival."

Then he turned to Mathilde and bowed over the hand she held out to him. Sebastian had come forward with a sudden return of his gracious and rather old-world manner.   He did not offer to shake hands, but bowed.

"A son of Louis d'Arragon who was fortunate enough to escape to England?" he inquired with a courteous gesture.

"The only son," replied the new-comer.

"I am honoured to make the acquaintance of Monsieur le Marquis," said Antoine Sebastian slowly.

"Oh, you must not call me that," replied D'Arragon with a short laugh. "I am an English sailor—that is all."

"And now, my dear Louis, I leave you," broke in Charles, who had rather impatiently awaited the end of these formalities. "A brief half-hour and I am with you again. You will stay here till I return."

He turned, nodded gaily to Désirée and ran downstairs.

Through the open windows they heard his quick, light footfall as he hurried up the Frauengasse. Something made them silent, listening to it.

It was not difficult to see that D'Arragon was a sailor. Not only had he the brown face of those who live in the open, but he had the silent, attentive air of one whose waking moments are a watch.

"You look at one as if one were the horizon," Désirée said to him long afterwards. But it was at this moment in the drawing-room in the Frauengasse that the comparison formed itself in her mind.

His face was rather narrow, with a square chin and straight lips. He was not quick in speech like Charles, but seemed to think before he spoke, with the result that he often appeared to be about to say something, and was interrupted before the words had been uttered.

"Unless my memory is a bad one, your mother was

an Englishwoman, monsieur," said Sebastian, " which
would account for your being in the English service."

"Not entirely," answered d'Arragon, "though my
mother was indeed English and died—in a French
prison. But it was from a sense of gratitude that my
father placed me in the English service—and I have
never regretted it, monsieur."

" Your father received kindnesses at English hands,
after his escape, like many others."

" Yes, and he was too old to repay them by doing
the country any service himself. He would have done
it if he could——"

D'Arragon paused, looking steadily at the tall old
man who listened to him with averted eyes.

"My father was one of those," he said at length,
" who did not think that in fighting for Bonaparte one
was necessarily fighting for France."

Sebastian held up a warning hand.

" In England——" he corrected, " in England one
may think such things. But not in France, and still
less in Dantzig."

" If one is an Englishman," replied D'Arragon with
a smile, " one may think them where one likes, and say
them when one is disposed. It is one of the privileges
of the nation, monsieur."

He made the statement lightly, seeing the humour
of it with a cosmopolitan understanding, without any

suggestion of the boastfulness of youth. Désirée noticed that his hair was turning grey at the temples.

"I did not know," he said, turning to her, "that Charles was in Dantzig, much less that he was celebrating so happy an occasion. We ran against each other by accident in the street. It was a lucky accident that allowed me to make your acquaintance so soon after you have become his wife."

"It scarcely seems possible that it should be an accident," said Désirée. "It must have been the work of fate—if fate has time to think of such an insignificant person as myself and so small an event as my marriage in these days."

"Fate," put in Mathilde in her composed voice and manner, "has come to Dantzig to-day."

"Ah!"

"Yes. You are the second unexpected arrival this afternoon."

D'Arragon turned and looked at Mathilde. His manner, always grave and attentive, was that of a reader who has found an interesting book on a dusty shelf.

"Has the Emperor come?" he asked.

Mathilde nodded.

"I thought I saw something in Charles's face," he said reflectively, looking back through the open door towards the stairs where Charles had nodded farewell to them. "So the Emperor is here, in Dantzig?"

He turned towards Sebastian, who stood with a stony face.

"Which means war," he said.

"It always means war," replied Sebastian in a tired voice. "Is he again going to prove himself stronger than any?"

"Some day he will make a mistake," said D'Arragon cheerfully. "And then will come the day of reckoning."

"Ah!" said Sebastian, with a shake of the head that seemed to indicate an account so one-sided that none could ever liquidate it. "You are young, monsieur. You are full of hope."

"I am not young—I am thirty-one—but I am, as you say, full of hope. I look to that day, Monsieur Sebastian."

"And in the mean time?" suggested the man who seemed but a shadow of some one standing apart and far away from the affairs of daily life.

"In the mean time one must play one's part," returned D'Arragon, with his almost inaudible laugh, "whatever it may be."

There was no foreboding in his voice; no second meaning in the words. He was open and simple and practical, like the life he led.

"Then you have a part to play, too," said Désirée, thinking of Charles, who had been called away at such an inopportune moment, and had gone without complaint. "It is the penalty we pay for living in one of the less dull periods of history. He touches your life too."

"He touches every one's life, mademoiselle. That is what makes him so great a man. Yes. I have a little part to play. I am like one of the unseen supernumeraries who has to see that a door is open to allow the great actors to make an effective *entrée*. I am lent to Russia for the war that is coming. It is a little part. I have to keep open one small portion of the line of communication between England and St. Petersburg, so that news may pass to and fro."

He glanced towards Mathilde as he spoke. She was listening with an odd eagerness which he noted, as he noted everything, methodically and surely. He remembered it afterwards.

"That will not be easy, with Denmark friendly to France," said Sebastian, "and every Prussian port closed to you."

"But Sweden will help. She is not friendly to France."

Sebastian laughed, and made a gesture with his white and elegant hand, of contempt and ridicule.

"And, *bon Dieu!* what a friendship it is," he exclaimed, "that is based on the fear of being taken for an enemy."

"It is a friendship that waits its time, monsieur," said D'Arragon taking up his hat.

"Then you have a ship, monsieur, here in the Baltic?" asked Mathilde with more haste than was characteristic of her usual utterance.

"A very small one, mademoiselle," he answered. "So small that I could turn her round here in the Frauengasse."

"But she is fast?"

"The fastest in the Baltic, mademoiselle," he answered. "And that is why I must take my leave —with the news you have told me."

He shook hands as he spoke, and bowed to Sebastian, whose generation was content with the more formal salutation. Désirée went to the door, and led the way downstairs.

"We have but one servant," she said, "who is busy."

On the doorstep he paused for a moment. And Désirée seemed to expect him to do so.

"Charles and I have always been like brothers— you will remember that always, will you not?"

"Yes," she answered with her gay nod. "I will remember."

"Then good-bye, mademoiselle."

"Madame," she corrected lightly.

"Madame, my cousin," he said, and departed smiling.

Désirée went slowly upstairs again.

CHAPTER IV.

THE CLOUDED MOON.

*Quand on se méfie on se trompe, quand on ne se méfie pas,
on est trompé.*

CHARLES DARRAGON had come to Dantzig a year earlier.
He was a lieutenant in an infantry regiment, and he
was twenty-five. Many of his contemporaries were
colonels in these days of quick promotion, when men
lived at such a rate that few of them lived long. But
Charles was too easy-going to envy any man.

When he arrived he knew no one in Dantzig, had
few friends in the army of occupation. In six months
he possessed acquaintances in every street, and was on
terms of easy familiarity with all his fellow-officers.

" If the army of occupation had more officers like
young Darragon," a town councillor had grimly said to
Rapp, " the Dantzigers would soon be resigned to your
presence."

It seemed that Charles had the gift of popularity.
He was open and hearty, hail-fellow-well-met with the
new-comers, who were numerous enough at this time,

quick to understand the quiet men, ready to make merry with the gay. Regarding himself, he was quite open and frank.

"I am a poor devil of a lieutenant," he said, "that is all."

Reserve is fatal to popularity: friendship cannot exist without it. Charles had, it seemed, nothing to hide, and was indifferent to the secrets of others. It is such people who receive many confidences.

"But it must go no farther . . ." a hundred men had said to him.

"My friend, by to-morrow I shall have forgotten all about it," he invariably replied, which men remembered afterwards and were glad.

A certain sort of friendship seemed to exist between Charles Darragon and Colonel de Casimir—not without patronage on one side and a slightly constraining sense of obligation on the other. It was de Casimir who had introduced Charles to Mathilde Sebastian at a formal reception at General Rapp's. Charles, of course, fell in love with Mathilde, and out again after half-an-hour's conversation. There was something cold and calculating about Mathilde which held him at arm's length with as much efficacy as the strictest duenna. Indeed, there are some maidens who require no better chaperon for their hearts than their own heads.

A few days after this introduction Charles met

Mathilde and Désirée in the Langgasse, and he fell in love with Désirée. He went about for a whole week seeking opportunity to tell her without delay what had happened to him. The opportunity presented itself before long; for one morning he saw her walking quickly towards the Kuh-brücke with her skates swinging from her wrist. It was a sunny, still, winter morning, such as temperate countries never know. Désirée's eyes were bright with youth and happiness. The cold air had slightly emphasized the rosy colour of her cheeks.

Charles caught his breath at the sight of her, though she did not happen to perceive him. He called a sleigh and drove to the barracks for his own skates. Then to the Kuh-brücke, where a reach of the Mottlau was cleared and kept in order for skating. He overpaid the sleigh-driver and laughed aloud at the man's boorish surprise. There was no one so happy as Charles Darragon in all the world. He was going to tell Désirée that he loved her.

At first Désirée was surprised, as was only natural. For she had not thought again of the pleasant young officer introduced to her by Mathilde. They had not even commented on him after he had made his gay bow and gone.

She had of course thought of these things in the abstract when her busy mind had nothing more material and immediate to consider. She had probably arranged how some abstract person should some day tell her of his love and how she should make reply. But she had never imagined the incident as it actually happened. She had never pictured a youth in a gay uniform looking down at her with ardent eyes as he skated by her side through the crisp still air, while the ice sang a high clear song beneath their feet in accompaniment to his hurried laughing words of protestation. He seemed to touch life lightly and to anticipate nothing but happiness. In truth, it was difficult to be tragic on such a morning.

These were the heedless days of the beginning of the century, when men not only threw away their lives, but played ducks-and-drakes with their chances of happiness in a manner quite incomprehensible to the careful method of human thought to-day. Charles Darragon lived only in the present moment. He was in love with her. Désirée must marry him.

It was quite different from what she had anticipated. She had looked forward to such a moment with a secret misgiving. The abstract person of her thoughts had always inspired her with a painful shyness and an indefinite, breathless fear. But the lover who was here now in the flesh by her side inspired none of these feelings. On the contrary, she felt easy and natural and quite at home with him. There was nothing alarming about his flushed face and laughing eyes. She was not at all afraid of him. She even felt in some vague way older than he, though he had just told her that he was twenty-five, and four years her senior.

She accepted the violets which he had hurriedly bought for her as he came through the Langenmarkt, but she would not say that she loved him, because she did not. She was in most ways quite a matter-of-fact person, and she was of an honest mind. She said she would think about it. She did not love him now—she knew that. She could not say that she would not learn to love him some day, but there seemed no likelihood of it at present. Then he would shoot himself! He would certainly shoot himself unless she learnt to love him! And she asked " When ? " and they both laughed. They changed the subject, but after a time they came back to it; which is the worst of love—one always comes back to it.

Then suddenly he began to assume an air of pro-prietorship, and burst into a hundred explanations of what fears he felt for her; for her happiness and welfare. Her father was absent-minded and heedless. He was not a fit guardian for her. Was she not the prettiest girl in all Dantzig—in all the world? Her sister was not fond enough of her to care for her properly. He announced his intention of seeing her father the next day. Everything should be done in order. Not a word must be hinted by the most watchful neighbour against the perfect propriety of their betrothal.

Désirée laughed and said that he was progressing rather rapidly. She had only her instinct to guide her through these troubled waters; which was much better than experience. Experience in a woman is tantamount to a previous conviction against a prisoner.

Charles was grave, however; a rare tribute. He was in love for the first time, which often makes men quite honest for a brief period—even unselfish. Of course, some men are honest and unselfish all their lives; which perhaps means that they remain in love —for the first time—all their lives. They are rare, of course. But the sort of woman with whom it is possible to remain in love all through a lifetime is rarer.

So Charles waylaid Antoine Sebastian the next day as he went out of the Frauenthor for his walk in the morning sun by the side of the frozen Mottlau. He was better received than he had any reason to expect.

"I am only a lieutenant," he said, "but in these days, monsieur, you know—— there are possibilities."

He laughed gaily as he waved his gloves in the direction of Russia, across the river. But Sebastian's face clouded, and Charles, who was quick and sympathetic, abandoned that point in his argument almost before the words were out of his lips.

"I have a little money," he said, "in addition to my pay. I assure you, monsieur, I am not of mean birth."

"You are an orphan?" said Sebastian curtly.

"Yes."

"Of the . . . Terror?"

"Yes; I—— well, one does not make much of one's parentage in these rough times—monsieur."

"Your father's name was Charles—like your own?"

"Yes."

"The second son?"

"Yes, monsieur. Did you know him?"

"One remembers a name here and there," answered Sebastian, in his stiff manner, looking straight in front of him.

"There was a tone in your voice——," began Charles, and, again perceiving that he was on a false scent, broke off abruptly. "If love can make mademoiselle happy——," he said; and a gesture of his right hand seemed to indicate that his passion was beyond the measure of words.

So Charles Darragon was permitted to pay his addresses to Désirée in the somewhat formal manner of a day which, upon careful consideration, will be found to have been no more foolish than the present. He made no inquiries respecting Désirée's parentage.

It was Désirée he wanted, and that was all. They understood the arts of love and war in the great days of the Empire.

The rest was easy enough, and the gods were kind. Charles had even succeeded in getting a month's leave of absence. They were to spend their honeymoon at Zoppot, a little fishing-village hidden in the pines by the Baltic shore, only eight miles from Dantzig, where the Vistula loses itself at last in the salt water.

All these arrangements had been made, as Désirée had prepared her trousseau, with a zest and gaiety which all were invited to enjoy. It is said that love is an egoist. Charles and Désirée had no desire to keep their happiness to themselves, but wore it, as it were, upon their sleeves.

The attitude of the Frauengasse towards Désirée's wedding was only characteristic of the period. Every house in Dantzig looked askance upon its neighbour at this time. Each roof covered a number of contending interests.

Some were for the French, and some for the conqueror's unwilling ally, William of Prussia. The names above the shops were German and Polish. There are to-day Scotch names also, here as elsewhere on the Baltic shores. When the serfs were liberated it was necessary to find surnames for these free men— these Pauls-the-son-of-Paul; and the nobles of Esthonia and Lithuania were reading Sir Walter Scott at the time.

The burghers of Dantzig ("They must be made to pay, these rich Dantzigers," wrote Napoleon to Rapp) trembled for their wealth, and stood aghast by their empty counting-houses; for their gods had been cast down; commerce was at a standstill. There were many, therefore, who hated the French, and cherished a secret love of those bluff British captains—so like themselves in build, and thought, and slowness of speech—who would thrash their wooden brigs through the shallow seas, despite decrees and threats and sloops-of-war, so long as they could lay them alongside the granaries of the Vistula. Lately the very tolls had been collected by a French customs service, and the wholesale smuggling, to which even Governor Rapp—that long-headed Alsatian—had closed his eyes, was at an end.

Again, the Poles who looked on Dantzig as the seaport of that great kingdom of Eastern Europe which was and is no more, had been assured that France would set up again the throne of the Jagellons and the Sobieskis. There was a Poniatowski high in the Emperor's service and esteem. The Poles were for France.

The Jew, hurrying along close by the wall—always in the shadow—traded with all and trusted none.

Who could tell what thoughts were hidden beneath the ragged fur cap—what revenge awaited its consummation in the heart crushed by oppression and contempt?

Besides these civilians there were many who had a military air within their civil garb. For the pendulum of war had swung right across from Cadiz to Dantzig, and swept northwards in its wake the merchants of death, the men who live by feeding soldiers and rifling the dead.

All these were in the streets, rubbing shoulders with the gay epaulettes of the Saxons, the Badeners, the Würtembergers, the Westphalians, and the Hessians, who had been poured into Dantzig by Napoleon during the months when he had continued to exchange courteous and affectionate letters with Alexander of Russia. For more than a year the broad-faced Bavarians (who have borne the brunt of every war in Central Europe) had been peaceably quartered in the town. Half a dozen different tongues were daily heard in this city of the plain, and no man knew who might be his friend and who his enemy. For some who were allies to-day were commanded by their kings to slay each other to-morrow.

In the wine-cellars and the humbler beer-shops, in the great houses of the councillors, and behind the snowy lace curtains of the Frauengasse and the Portchaisengasse a thousand slow Northerners spoke of these things and kept them in their hearts. A hundred secret societies passed from mouth to mouth instruction, warning, encouragement. Germany has always been the home of the secret society. Northern Europe gave birth to those countless associations which have proved stronger than kings and surer than a throne. The Hanseatic League, the first of the commercial unions which were destined to build up the greatest empire of the world, lived longest in Dantzig.

The Tugendbund, men whispered, was not dead but sleeping. Napoleon, who had crushed it once, was watching for its revival; had a whole army of his matchless secret police ready for it. And the Tugendbund had had its centre in Dantzig.

Perhaps, in the Rathskeller itself—one of the largest wine stores in the world, where tables and chairs are set beneath the arches of the Exchange, a vast cave under the streets—perhaps here the Tugendbund still encouraged men to be virtuous and self-denying, for no other or higher purpose than the overthrow of the Scourge of Europe. Here the richer citizens have met from time immemorial to drink with solemnity and a decent leisure the wines sent hither in their own ships from the Rhine, from Greece and the Crimea, from Bordeaux and Burgundy, from the Champagne and Tokay. This is not only the Rathskeller, but the real Rathlaus, where the Dantzigers have taken counsel over their afternoon wine from generation to generation, whence have been issued to all the world those decrees of probity and a commercial uprightness between buyer and seller, debtor and creditor, master and man, which reached to every corner of the commercial world. And now it was whispered that the latter-day Dantzigers—the sons of those who formed the Hanseatic League: mostly fat men with large faces and shrewd, calculating eyes; high foreheads; good solid men, who knew the world, and how to make their way in it; withal, good judges of a wine and great drinkers, like that William the Silent, who braved and met and conquered the European scourge of mediæval times—it was whispered that these were reviving the Tugendbund.

Amid such contending interests, and in a free city so near to several frontiers, men came and went without attracting undesired attention. Each party suspected a new-comer of belonging to the other.

"He scrapes a fiddle," Koch had explained to the inquiring fishwife. And perhaps he knew no more than this of Antoine Sebastian. Sebastian was poor. All the Frauengasse knew that. But the Frauengasse itself was poor, and no man in Dantzig was so foolish at this time as to admit that he had possessions.

This was, moreover, not the day of display or

snobbery. The king of snobs, Louis XVI., had died to some purpose, for a wave of manliness had swept across human thought at the beginning of the century. The world has rarely been the poorer for the demise of a Bourbon.

The Frauengasse knew that Antoine Sebastian played the fiddle to gain his daily bread, while his two daughters taught dancing for that same safest and most satisfactory of all motives.

"But he holds his head so high!" once observed the stout and matter-of-fact daughter of a Councillor. "Why has he that grand manner?"

"Because he is a dancing-master," replied Désirée, with a grave assurance. "He does it so that you may copy him. Chin up. Oh! how fat you are."

Désirée herself was slim enough and as yet only half grown. She did not dance so well as Mathilde, who moved through a quadrille with the air of a duchess, and threw into a polonaise or mazurka a quiet grace which was the envy and despair of her pupils. Mathilde was patient with the slow and heavy of foot, while Désirée told them bluntly that they were fat. Nevertheless, they were afraid of Mathilde, and only laughed at Désirée when she rushed angrily at them, and, seizing them by the arms, danced them round the room with the energy of despair.

Sebastian, who had an oddly judicial air, such as

men acquire who are in authority, held the balance
evenly between the sisters, and smiled apologetically
over his fiddle towards the victim of Désirées im-
petuosity.

"Yes," he would reply to watching mothers, who
tried to lead him to say that their daughter was the
best dancer in the school: "Yes, Mathilde puts it into
their heads, and Désirée shakes it down to their feet."

In all matters of the household Désirée played a
similar part. She was up early and still astir after
nine o'clock at night, when the other houses in the
Frauengasse were quiet, if there were work to do.

"It is because she has no method," said Mathilde,
who had herself a well-ordered mind, and that quickness which never needs to hurry.

CHAPTER V.

THE WEISSEN RÖSS'L.

The moth will singe her wings, and singed return,
Her love of light quenching her fear of pain.

THERE are quite a number of people who get through life without realizing their own insignificance. Ninety-nine out of a hundred persons signify nothing, and the hundredth is usually so absorbed in the message which he has been sent into the world to deliver that he loses sight of the messenger altogether.

By a merciful dispensation of Providence we are permitted to bustle about in our immediate little circle like the ant, running hither and thither with all the sublime conceit of that insect. We pick up, as he does, a burden which on close inspection will be found to be absolutely valueless, something that somebody else has thrown away. We hoist it over obstructions while there is usually a short way round; we fret and sweat and fume. Then we drop the burden and rush off at a tangent to pick up another. We write letters to our friends explaining to them what we are about.

E

We even indite diaries to be read by goodness knows whom, explaining to ourselves what we have been doing. Sometimes we find something that really looks valuable, and rush to our particular ant-heap with it while our neighbours pause and watch us. But they really do not care; and if the rumour of our discovery reach so far as the next ant-heap, the bustlers there are almost indifferent, though a few may feel a passing pang of jealousy. They may perhaps remember our name, and will soon forget what we discovered—which is Fame. While we are falling over each other to attain this, and dying to tell each other what it feels like when we have it, or think we have it, let us pause for a moment and think of an ant—who kept a diary.

Désirée did not keep a diary. Her life was too busy for ink. She had had to work for her daily bread, which is better than riches. Her life had been full of occupation from morning till night, and God had given her sleep from night till morning. It is better to work for others than to think for them. Some day the world will learn to have a greater respect for the workers than for the thinkers, who are idle, wordy persons, frequently thinking wrong.

Désirée remembered the siege and the occupation of Dantzig by French troops. She was at school in the Jopengasse when the Treaty of Tilsit—that peace which was nothing but a pause—was concluded. She had seen Luisa of Prussia, the good Queen who baffled Napoleon. Her childhood had passed away in the roar of siege-guns. Her girlhood, in the Frauengasse, had been marked by the various woes of Prussia, by each successive step in the development of Napoleon's ambition. There were no bogey-men in the night-nursery at the beginning of the century. One Aaron's rod of a bogey had swallowed all the rest, and children buried their sobs in the pillow for fear of Napoleon. There were no ghosts in the dark corners of the stairs when Désirée, candle in hand, went to bed at eight o'clock, half an hour before Mathilde. The shadows on the wall were the shadows of soldiers—the wind roaring in the chimney was like the sound of distant cannon. When the timid glanced over their shoulders, the apparition they looked for was that of a little man in a cocked hat and a long grey coat.

This was not an age in which the individual life was highly valued. Men were great to-day and gone to-morrow. Women were of small account. It was the day of deeds and not of words. In these latter times all that is changed, and the talker has a hearing.

Désirée had never been oppressed by a sense of her own importance, which oppression leaves its mark on many a woman's face in these times. She had not, it would seem, expected much from life; and when much was given to her she received it without misgivings. She was young and light-hearted, and she lived in a reckless age.

She was not surprised when Charles failed to return. The chaise that was to carry them to Zoppot stood in the Frauengasse on the shady side of the street in the heat of the afternoon for more than an hour. Then she ran out and told the driver to go back to his stables.

"One cannot go for a honeymoon alone," she explained airily to her father, who was peevish and restless, standing by the window with the air of one who expects without knowing what to expect. "It is, at all events, quite clear that there is nothing for me to do but wait."

She made light of it, and laughed at her father's grave face. Mathilde said nothing, but her silence seemed to suggest that this was no more than she had foretold, or at all events foreseen. She was too proud or too generous to put her thoughts into words. For pride and generosity are often confounded. There are many who give because they are too proud to withhold.

Désirée got her needlework and sat by the open window awaiting Charles. She could hear the continuous clatter of carts on the quay, and the voices of the men working in the great granaries across the river.

The whole city seemed to be astir, and men hurried to and fro in even the quiet Frauengasse, while the clatter of cavalry and the heavy rumble of gun-carriages could be heard over the roofs from the direction of the Langenmarkt. There was a sense of hurry in the dusty air. The Emperor had arrived, and the magic of his name lifted men out of themselves. It seemed nothing extraordinary to Désirée that her life should be taken up by this whirlwind, and carried on she knew not whither.

At dinner-time Charles had not returned. Antoine Sebastian dined at half-past four, in the manner of Northern Europe; but his daughters provided his table with the lighter meats of France, which he preferred to the German cuisine. Sebastian's dinner was an event in the day, though he ate sparingly enough, and found a mental rather than a physical pleasure in the ceremonious sequence of courses.

It was now too late to think of going to Zoppot. After dinner Mathilde and Désirée prepared the rooms which had been destined for the occupation of the married pair after the honeymoon.

"We shall have to omit Zoppot, that is all," said Désirée cheerfully, and fell to unpacking the bridal clothes which had been so merrily laid in the trunks.

At half-past six a soldier brought a hurried note from Charles.

"I cannot return to-night, as I am about to start for Königsberg," he wrote. "It is a commission which I could not refuse if I wished to. You, I know, would have me go and do my duty."

There was more which Désirée did not read aloud. Charles had always found it easy enough to tell Désirée how much he loved her, and was gaily indifferent to the ears of others. But she seemed to be restrained by some feeling which had found birth in her heart during her wedding-day. She said nothing of Charles's protestations of love.

"Decidedly," she said, folding the letter, and placing it in her work-basket. "Fate is interfering in our affairs to-day."

She turned to her work again without further complaint, almost with a sense of relief. Mathilde, whose steady grey eyes saw everything, penetrating every thought, glanced at her with a suddenly aroused interest. Désirée herself was half surprised at the philosophy with which she met this fresh misfortune.

Antoine Sebastian had never acquired the habit of drinking tea in the evening, which had found favour in these northern countries bordering on Russia. Instead, he usually went out at this time to one of the many wine-rooms or Bier Halles in the town to drink a slow and meditative glass of beer with such friends as he had made in Dantzig. For he was a lonely man, whose face was quite familiar to many who looked for a bow or a friendly salutation in vain.

If he went to the Rathskeller it was on the invitation of a friend; for he could not afford to pay the vintage of that cellar, though he drank the wine with the slow mouthing of a connoisseur when he had it.

More often than not he took a walk first, passing out of the Frauenthor on to the quay, where he turned to left or right and made his way back through one or other of the town gates, by devious narrow streets, to that which is still called the Portchaisengasse, though chairs and carriers have long ceased to pass along it. Here, on the northern side of the street is an old inn, "Zum weissen Röss'l," with a broken, ill-carved head of a white horse above the door. Across the face of the house is written, in old German letters, an invitation :

> Gruss Gott. Tritt ein!
> Bring Glück herein.

But few seemed to accept it. Even a hundred years ago the White Horse was behind the times, and fashion sought the wider streets.

Antoine Sebastian was perhaps ashamed of frequenting so humble a house of entertainment, where for a groschen he could have a glass of beer. He seemed to make his way through the narrower streets for some purpose, changing his route from day to day, and hurrying across the wider thoroughfares with the air of one desirous to attract but little attention. He was not alone in the quiet streets, for there were many in Dantzig at this time who from wealth had fallen to want. Many counting-houses once noisy with prosperity were now closed and silent. For five years the prosperous Dantzig had lain crushed beneath the iron heel of the conqueror.

It would seem that Sebastian had only waited for the explanation of Charles's most ill-timed absence to carry out his usual programme. The clock in the tower of the Rathhaus had barely struck seven when he took his hat and cloak from the peg near the dining-room door. He was so absorbed that he did not perceive Papa Barlasch seated just within the open door of the kitchen. But Barlasch saw him, and scratched his head at the sight.

The northern evenings are chill even in June, and Sebastian fumbled with his cloak. It would appear that he was little used to helping himself in such matters. Barlasch came out of the kitchen when Sebastian's back was turned and helped him to put the flowing cloak straight upon his shoulders.

"Thank you, Lisa, thank you," said Sebastian in German, without looking round. By accident Barlasch had performed one of Lisa's duties, and the master of the house was too deeply engaged in thought to notice any difference in the handling or to perceive the smell of snuff that heralded the approach of Papa Barlasch.

Sebastian took his hat and went out closing the door behind him, and leaving Barlasch, who had followed him to the door, standing rather stupidly on the mat.

"Absent-minded—the citizen," muttered Barlash, returning to the kitchen, where he resumed his seat on a chair by the open door. He scratched his head and appeared to lapse into thought. But his brain was slow as were his movements. He had been drinking to the health of the bride. He thumped himself on the brow with his closed fist.

"Sacred-name-of-a-thunderstorm," he said. "Where have I seen that face before?"

Sebastian went out by the Frauenthor to the quay. Although it was dusk, the granaries were still at work. The river was full of craft and the roadway choked by rows and rows of carts, all of one pattern, too big and too heavy for roads that are laid across a marsh.

He turned to the right, but found his way blocked at the corner of the Langenmarkt, where the road narrows to pass under the Grünes Thor. Here the idlers of the evening hour were collected in a crowd, peering over each other's shoulders towards the roadway and the bridge. Sebastian was a tall man, and had no need to stand on tip-toe in order to see the straight rows of bayonets swinging past, and the line of shakos rising and falling in unison with the beat of a thousand feet on the hollow woodwork of the drawbridge.

The troops had been passing out of the city all the afternoon on the road to Elbing and Königsberg.

"It is the same," said a man standing near to Sebastian, "at the Hohes Thor, where they are marching out by the road leading to Königsberg by way of Dessau."

"It is farther than Königsberg that they are going," was the significant answer of a white-haired veteran who had probably been at Eylau, for he had a crushed look.

"But war is not declared," said the first speaker.

"Does that matter?"

And both turned towards Sebastian with the challenging air that invites opinion or calls for admiration of uncommon shrewdness. He was better clad than they. He must know more than they did. But Sebastian looked over their heads and did not seem to have heard their conversation.

He turned back and went another way, by side streets and the little narrow alleys that nearly always encircle a cathedral, and are still to be found on all sides of the Marienkirche. At last he came to the Portchaisengasse, which was quiet enough in the twilight, though he could hear the tramp of soldiers along the Langgasse and the rumble of the guns.

There were only two lamps in the Portchaisengasse, swinging on wrought-iron gibbets at each end of the street. These were not yet alight, though the day was fading fast, and the western light could scarcely find its way between the high gables which hung over the road and seemed to lean confidentially towards each other.

Sebastian was going towards the door of the Weissen Röss'l when some one came out of the hostelry, as if he had been awaiting him within the porch.

The new-comer, who was a fat man with baggy cheeks and odd, light blue eyes—the eyes of an enthusiast, one would say—passed Sebastian, making a little gesture which at once recommended silence, and bade him turn and follow. At the entrance to a little alley leading down towards the Marienkirche the fat man awaited Sebastian, whose pace had not quickened, nor had his walk lost any of its dignity.

"Not there to-night," said the man, holding up a thick forefinger and shaking it sideways.

"Then where?"

"Nowhere to-night," was the answer. "He has come—you know that?"

"Yes," answered Sebastian slowly, "for I saw him."

"He is at supper now with Rapp and the others. The town is full of his people. His spies are every-where. There are two in the Weissen Röss'l who

pretend to be Bavarians. See! There is another—
just there."

He pointed the thick forefinger down the Portchaisengasse where it widens to meet the Langgasse,
where the last remains of daylight, reflected to and fro
between the houses, found freer play than in the narrow
alley where they stood.

Sebastian looked in the direction indicated. An
officer was walking away from them. A quick observer
would have noticed that his spurs made no noise, and
that he carried his sword instead of allowing it to
clatter after him. It was not clear whence he had
come. It must have been from a doorway nearly
opposite to the Weissen Röss'l.

"I know that man," said Sebastian.

"So do I," was the reply. "It is Colonel de
Casimir."

With a little nod the fat man went out again into
the Portchaisengasse in the direction of the inn, as if he
were keeping watch there.

CHAPTER VI.

THE SHOEMAKER OF KÖNIGSBERG.

Chacun ne comprend que ce qu'il trouve en soi.

NEARLY two years had passed since the death of Queen Luisa of Prussia. And she from her grave yet spake to her people—as sixty years later she was destined to speak to another King of Prussia, who said a prayer by her tomb before departing on a journey that was to end in Fontainebleau with an imperial crown and the reckoning for all time of the seven years of woe that followed Tilsit and killed a queen.

Two years earlier than that, in 1808, while Luisa yet lived, a few scientists and professors of Königsberg had formed a sort of Union—vague enough and visionary—to encourage virtue and discipline and patriotism. And now, in 1812, four years later, the memory of Luisa still lingered in those narrow streets that run by the banks of the Pregel beneath the great castle of Königsberg, while the Tugendbund, like a seed that has been crushed beneath an iron heel, had spread its roots underground.

From Dantzig, the commercial, to Königsberg, the kingly and the learned, the tide of war rolled steadily onwards. It is a tide that carries before it a certain flotsam of quick and active men, keen-eyed, restless, rising—men who speak with a sharp authority and pay from a bottomless purse. The arrival of Napoleon in Dantzig swept the first of the tide on to Königsberg.

Already every house was full. The high-gabled warehouses on the riverside could not be used for barracks, for they too had been crammed from floor to roof with stores and arms. So the soldiers slept where they could. They bivouacked in the timber-yards by the riverside. The country-women found the Neuer Markt transformed into a camp when they brought their baskets in the early morning, but they met with eager buyers, who haggled laughingly in half a dozen different tongues. There was no lack of money, however.

Cartloads of it were on the road.

The Neuer Markt in Königsberg is a square, of which the lower side is a quay on the Pregel. The river is narrow here. Across it the country is open. The houses surrounding the quadrangle are all alike—two-storied buildings with dormer windows in the

roof. There are trees in front. In front of that
which is now Number Thirteen, at the right-hand
corner, facing west, sideways to the river, the trees
grow quite close to the windows, so that an active
man or a boy might without great risk leap from the
eaves below the dormer window into the topmost
branches of the linden, which here grows strong
and tough, as it surely should do in the fatherland.

A young soldier, seeking lodgings, who happened
to knock at the door of Number Thirteen less than
thirty hours after the arrival of Napoleon at Dantzig,
looked upward through the shady boughs, and noted
their growth with the light of interest in his eye.
It would almost seem that the house had been
described to him as that one in the Neuer Markt
against which the lindens grew. For he had walked
all round the square between the trees and houses
before knocking at this door, which bore no number
then, as it does to-day.

His tired horse had followed him meditatively,
and now stood with drooping head in the shade. The
man himself wore a dark uniform, white with dust.
His hair was dusty and rather lank. He was not a
very tidy soldier.

He stood looking at the sign which swung from
the doorpost, a relic of the Polish days. It bore the

painted semblance of a boot. For in Poland—a frontier country, as in frontier cities where many tongues are heard—it is the custom to paint a picture rather than write a word. So that every house bears the sign of its inmate's craft, legible alike to Lithuanian or Ruthenian, Swede or Cossack of the Don.

He knocked again, and at last the door was opened by a thickly-built man, who looked, not at his face, but at his boots. As these wanted no repair he half closed the door again and looked at the new-comer's face.

"What do you want?" he asked.

"A lodging."

The door was almost closed, when the soldier made an odd and, as it would seem, tentative gesture with his left hand. All the fingers were clenched, and with his extended thumb he scratched his chin slowly from side to side.

"I have no lodging to let," said the bootmaker. But he did not shut the door.

"I can pay," said the other, with his thumb still at his chin. He had quick, blue eyes beneath the shaggy hair that wanted cutting. "I am very tired—it is only for one night."

"Who are you?" asked the bootmaker.

The soldier was a dull and slow man. He leant

against the doorpost with tired gestures before replying.

"Sergeant in a Schleswig regiment, in charge of spare horses."

"And you have come far?"

"From Dantzig without a halt."

The shoemaker looked him up and down with a doubting eye, as if there were something about him that was not quite clear and above-board. The dust and fatigue were, however, unmistakable.

"Who sent you to me, anyway?" he grumbled.

"Oh, I do not know," was the half-impatient answer; "the man I lodged with in Dantzig or another, I forget. It was Koch the locksmith in the Schmiedegasse. See, I have money. I tell you it is for one night. Say yes or no. I want to get to bed and to sleep."

"How much do you pay?"

"A thaler—if you like. Among friends, one is willing to pay."

After a short minute of hesitation the shoemaker opened the door wider and came out.

"And there will be another thaler for the horse, which I shall have to take to the stable of the wood-merchant at the corner. Go into the workshop and sit down till I come."

He stood in the doorway and watched the soldier

F

seat himself wearily on a bench in the workshop among the ancient boots, past repair, one would think, and lean his head against the wall.

He was half asleep already, and the bootmaker, who was lame, shrugged his shoulders as he led away the tired horse, with a gesture half of pity, half of doubting suspicion. Had it suggested itself to his mind, and had it been within the power of one so halt and heavy-footed to turn back noiselessly, he would have found his visitor wide-awake enough, hurriedly opening every drawer and peering under the twine and needles, lifting every bale of leather, shaking out the very boots awaiting repair.

When the dweller in Number Thirteen returned, the soldier was asleep, and had to be shaken before he would open his eyes.

" Will you eat before you go to bed ? " asked the bootmaker not unkindly.

" I ate as I came along the street," was the reply. " No, I will go to bed. What time is it ? "

" It is only seven o'clock—but no matter."

" No, it is no matter. To-morrow I must be astir by five."

" Good," said the shoemaker. " But you will get your money's worth. The bed is a good one. It is my son's. He is away, and I am alone in the house."

He led the way upstairs as he spoke, going heavily one step at a time, so that the whole house seemed to shake beneath his tread. The room was that attic in the roof which has a dormer window overhanging the linden tree. It was small and not too clean; for Königsberg was once a Polish city, and is not far from the Russian frontier.

The soldier hardly noticed his surroundings, but sat down instantly, with the abandonment of a shepherd's dog at the day's end.

"I will put a stitch in your boots for you while you sleep," said the host casually. "The thread is rotten, I can see. Look here—and here!"

He stooped, and with a quick turn of the awl which he carried in his belt he snapped the sewing at the join of the leg and the upper leather, bringing the frayed ends of the thread out to view.

Without answering, the soldier looked round for the boot-jack, lacking which, no German or Polish bedroom is complete.

When the bootmaker had gone, carrying the boots under his arm, the soldier, left to himself, made a grimace at the closed door. Without boots he was a prisoner in the house. He could hear his host at work already, downstairs in the shop, of which the door opened to the stairs and allowed passage to that smell of leather which breeds Radical convictions.

The regular "tap-tap" of the cobbler's hammer continued for an hour until dusk, and all the while the soldier lay dressed on his bed. Soon after, a creaking of the stairs told of the surreptitious approach of the unwilling host. He listened outside, and even tried the door, but found it bolted. The soldier, open-eyed on the bed, snored aloud. At the sound of the key on the outside of the door he made a grimace again. His features were very mobile, for Schleswig.

He heard the bootmaker descend the stairs again almost noiselessly, and, rising from the bed, he took his station at the window. All the Langgasse would seem to be eating-houses. The basement, which has a separate door, gives forth odours of simple Pomeranian meats, and every other house bears to this day the curt but comforting inscription, "Here one eats." It was only to be supposed that the bootmaker at the end of his day would repair for supper to some special haunt near by.

But the smell of cooking mingling with that of leather told that he was preparing his own evening meal. He was, it seemed, an unsociable man, who had but a son beneath his roof, and mostly lived alone.

Seated near the window, where the sunset light yet lingered, the Schleswiger opened his haversack, which was well supplied, and finding paper, pens and ink, fell to writing with one eye watchful of the window and both ears listening for any movement in the room below.

He wrote easily with a running pen, and sometimes he smiled as he wrote. More than once he paused and looked across the Neuer Markt above the trees and the roofs, towards the western sky, with a sudden grave wistfulness. He was thinking of some one in the west. It was assuredly not of war that this soldier wrote. Then, again, his attention would be attracted to some passer in the street below. He only gave half of his attention to his letter. He was, it seemed, a man who as yet touched life lightly; for he was quite young. But, nevertheless, his pen, urged by only half a mind that had all the energy of spring, flew over the paper. Sowing is so much easier than reaping.

Suddenly he threw his pen aside and moved quickly to the window which stood open. The shoemaker had gone out, closing the door softly behind him.

It was to be expected that he would turn to the left, upwards towards the town and the Langgasse, but it was in the direction of the river that his footsteps died away. There was no outlet on that side except by boat.

It was almost dark now, and the trees growing close to the window obscured the view. So eager was the lodger to follow the movements of his landlord that he crept in stocking-feet out on to the roof. By lying on his face below the window he could just distinguish the shadowy form of a lame man by the river edge. He was moving to and fro, unchaining a boat moored to the steps, which are more used in winter when the Pregel is a frozen roadway than in summer. There was no one else in the Neuer Markt, for it was the supper hour.

Out in the middle of the river a few ships were moored: high-prowed, square-sterned vessels of a Dutch build trading in the Frische Haaf and in the Baltic.

The soldier saw the boat steal out towards them. There was no other boat at the steps or in sight. He stood up on the edge of the roof, and after carefully measuring his distance, with quick eyes aglow with excitement, he leapt lightly across the leafy space into the topmost boughs, where he alighted in a forked branch almost without sound.

At dawn the next morning, while the shoemaker still slept, the soldier was astir again. He shivered as he rose, and went to the window, where his clothes were hanging from a rafter. The water was still dripping from them. Wrapt in a blanket he sat down by the open window to write while the morning air should dry his clothes.

That which he wrote was a long report—sheet after sheet closely written. And in the middle of his work he broke off to read again the letter that he had written the night before. With a quick, impulsive gesture he kissed the name it bore. Then he turned to his work again.

The sun was up before he folded the papers together. By way of a postscript he wrote a brief letter.

"DEAR C.—I have been fortunate, as you will see from the enclosed report. His Majesty cannot again say that I have been neglectful. I was quite right. It is Sebastian and only Sebastian that we need fear. Here they are clumsy conspirators compared to him. I have been in the river half the night listening at the open stern-window of a Reval pink to every word they said. His Majesty can safely come to Königsberg. Indeed, he is better out of Dantzig. For the whole country is riddled with that which they call patriotism, and we treason. But I can only repeat what his Majesty disbelieved the day before yesterday—that the heart of the ill is Dantzig, and the venom of it Sebastian. Who he really is and what he is about you must find out how you can. I go forward to-day to Gumbinnen. The enclosed letter to its address, I beg of you, if only in acknowledgment of all that I have sacrificed."

The letter was unsigned, and bore the date, "Dawn, June 10." This and the report, and that other letter (carefully sealed with a wafer) which did not deal with war or its alarms, were all placed in one large envelope.

He did not seal it, however, but sat thinking while the sun began to shine on the opposite houses. Then he withdrew the open letter, and added a postscript to it

"If an attempt were made on N.'s life—I should say Sebastian. If Prussia were to play us false suddenly, and cut us off from France—I should say nothing else than Sebastian. He is more dangerous than a fanatic; for he is too clever to be one."

The writer shivered and laughed in sheer amusement at his own misery as he drew on his wet clothes. The shoemaker was already astir, and presently knocked at his door.

"Yes, yes," the soldier cried, "I am astir."

And as his host rattled the door he opened it. He had unrolled his long cavalry cloak, and wore it over his wet clothes.

"You never told me your name," said the shoemaker. A suspicious man is always more suspicious at the beginning of the day.

"My name," answered the other carelessly. "Oh! my name is Max Brunner."

CHAPTER VII.

THE WAY OF LOVE.

Celui qui souffle le feu s'expose à être brûlé par les étincelles.

IT was said that Colonel de Casimir—that guest whose presence and uniform lent an air of distinction to the quiet wedding in the Frauengasse—was a Pole from Cracow. Men also whispered that he was in the confidence of the Emperor. But this must only have been a manner of speaking. For no man was ever admitted fully into the thoughts of that superhuman mind.

De Casimir was left behind in Dantzig when the army moved forward.

"There will be a great battle," he said, "somewhere near Vilna—and I shall miss it."

Indeed, every man was striving to get to the front. He who, himself, had given a new meaning to human ambition seemed able to inspire not only Frenchmen but soldiers of every nationality with fire from his own consuming flame.

"Yes! madame," said de Casimir; for it was to

Désirée that he spoke, "and your husband is more fortunate than I. He is sure of a staff appointment. He will be among the first. It will soon be over. To-morrow war is to be declared."

They were in the street—not far from the Frauengasse, whence Désirée, always practical, was hurrying towards the market-place. De Casimir had seemed idle until he perceived her.

Désirée made a little movement of horror at the announcement. She did not know that the fighting had already begun.

"Ah!" cried de Casimir with a reassuring smile. "You must be of good cheer. There will be no war at all. I tell you that in confidence. Russia will be paralyzed. I was going towards the Frauengasse when I perceived you; to pay my respects to your father, to say a word to you. Come—you are smiling again. That is right. You were so grave, madame, as you hurried along with your eyes looking far away. You must not think of Charles, if the thoughts make you look as you looked then."

His manner was kind and confidential and easy—inviting in response that which the confidential always expect, a return in kind. It is either hit or miss with such people; and de Casimir missed. He saw Désirée draw back. She was young, and of that clear fairness of skin which seems to let the thoughts out through

the face so that any can read them. That which her
face expressed at that moment was a clear and definite
refusal to confide anything whatsoever in this little
dark man who stood in front of her, looking into her
eyes with a deferential and sympathetic glance.

"I know for certain," he said, "that Charles was
well two days ago, and that he is highly thought of in
high quarters. I can tell you that, at all events."

"Thank you," said Désirée. She had nothing
against de Casimir. She had only seen him once or
twice, and she knew him to be Charles's friend, and in
some sense his patron. For de Casimir held a high
position in Dantzig. She was quite ready to like him
since Charles liked him; but she intended to do so at
her own range. It is always the woman who measures
the distance.

Désirée made a little movement as if to continue on
her way; and de Casimir instantly stood aside, with
a bow.

"Shall I find your father at home?" he asked.

"I think so. He was at home when I left," she
answered, responding to his salute with a friendly
nod.

De Casimir watched her go and stood for a moment
in reflection, as if going over in his mind that which
had passed between them.

"I must try the other one," he said to himself as

he turned down the Pfaffengasse. He continued his
way at a leisurely pace. At the corner of the Frauengasse he lingered in the shadow of the linden trees,
and while so doing saw Antoine Sebastian quit the
door of No 36, going in the opposite direction towards
the river, and pass out through the Frauenthor on to
the quay.

He made a little gesture of annoyance on being
told by the servant that Sebastian was out. After
a moment's reflection, he seemed to make up his mind
to ignore the conventionalities.

"It is merely," he said in his friendly and confidential manner to the servant, in perfect German,
"that I have news from Monsieur Darragon, the
husband of Mademoiselle Désirée. Madame is out—
you say. Well, then, what is to be done?"

He had a most charming, grave manner of asking
advice which few could resist.

The servant nodded at him with a twinkle of understanding in her eye.

"There is Fräulein Mathilde."

"But . . . well, ask her if she will do me the
honour of speaking to me for an instant. I leave it
to you. . . ."

"But come in," protested the servant. "Come
upstairs She will see you ; why not ?"

And she led the way upstairs. Papa Barlasch,

sitting just within the kitchen door, where he sat all day doing nothing, glanced upwards through his over-hanging eyebrows at the clink of spurs and the clatter of de Casimir's sword against the banisters. He had the air of a watchdog.

Mathilde was not in the drawing-room, and the servant left the visitor there alone, saying that she would seek her mistress. There were one or two books on the tables. One table was rather untidy; it was Désirée's. A writing-desk stood in the corner of the room. It was locked—and the lock was a good one. De Casimir was an observant man. He had time to make this observation, and to see that there were no letters in Désirée's work-basket; to note the titles of the books and the absence of name on the flyleaf, and was looking out of the window when the door opened and Mathilde came in.

This was a day when women were treated with a great show of deference, while in reality they had but little voice in the world's affairs. De Casimir's bow was deeper and more elaborate than would be con-sidered polite to-day. On standing erect he quickly suppressed a glance of surprise.

Mathilde must have expected him. She was dressed in white, and her hair was tied with a bright ribbon. In her cheeks, usually so pale, was a little touch of colour. It may have been because Désirée was not near, but de Casimir had never known until this moment how pretty Mathilde really was. There was something in her eyes, too, which gripped his attention. He remembered that at the wedding he had never seen her eyes. They had always been averted. But now they met his with a troubling directness.

De Casimir had a gallant manner. All women commanded his eager respect, which they could assess at such value as their fancy painted, remembering that it is for the woman to measure the distance. On the few occasions of previous encounters, de Casimir had been *empressé* in his manner towards Mathilde. As he looked at her, his quick mind ran back to former meetings. He had no recollection of having actually made love to her.

"Mademoiselle," he said, "for a soldier—in time of war—the conventions may, perhaps, be slightly relaxed. I was told that you were alone—that your father is out, and yet I persisted—— "

He spread out his hands and laughed appealingly, begging her, it would seem, to help him out of the social difficulty in which he found himself.

"My father will be sorry—— " she began.

"That is hardly the question," he interrupted; "I was thinking of your displeasure. But I have an excuse, I assure you. I only ask a moment to tell you that I have heard from Konigsberg that Charles

Darragon is in good health there, and is moving forward with the advance-guard to the frontier."

"You are kind to come so soon," answered Mathilde, and there was an odd note of disappointment in her voice. De Casimir must have heard it, for he glanced at her again with a gleam of surprise in his eyes.

"That is my excuse, Mademoiselle," he said with a tentative emphasis, as if he were feeling his way. He was an opportunist with all the quickness of one who must live by his wits among others existing on the same uncertain fare. He saw her flush, and again he hesitated as a wayfarer may hesitate when he finds an easy road where he had expected to climb a hill. What was the meaning of it? he seemed to ask himself.

"Charles does not interest you so much as he interests your sister?" he suggested.

"He has never interested me much," she replied indifferently. She did not ask him to sit down. It would not have been etiquette in an age when women were by some odd misjudgment considered incapable of managing their own hearts.

"Is that because he is in love, Mademoiselle?" inquired de Casimir with a guarded laugh.

"Perhaps so."

She did not look at him. De Casimir had not

missed this time. His air of candid confidence had met with a quick response He laughed again and moved towards the door. Mathilde stood motionless, and although she said no word, nor by any gesture bade him stay, he stopped on the threshold and turned again towards her.

"It was my conscience," he said, looking at her over his shoulder, "that bade me go."

Her face and her averted eyes asked why, but her straight lips were silent.

"Because I cannot claim to be more interesting than Charles Darragon," he hazarded. "And you, Mademoiselle, confess that you have no tolerance for a man who is in love."

"I have no tolerance for a man who is weakened by love. He should be strengthened and hardened by it."

"To —— ?"

"To do a man's work in the world," said Mathilde coldly.

De Casimir was standing by the open door. He closed it with his foot. He was professedly a man alert for the chance of a moment, which he was content to grasp without pausing to look ahead. Should there be difficulties yet unperceived, these in turn might present an opportunity to be seized by the quick-witted.

"Then you would admit, Mademoiselle," he said gravely, "that there may be good in a love that fights continually against ambition, and—does not prevail."

Mathilde did not answer at once. There was an odd suggestion of antagonism in their attitude towards each other—not irreconcilable, the poets tell us, with love—but this is assuredly not the Love that comes from Heaven and will go back there to live through eternity.

"Yes," said she at length.

"Such is my love for you," he said, his quick instinct telling him that with Mathilde few words were best.

He only spoke the thoughts of his age; for ambition was the ruling passion in men's hearts at this time. All who served the Great Adventurer gave it the first place in their consideration, and de Casimir only aped his betters. Though oddly enough the only two of all the great leaders who were to emerge still greater from the coming war—Ney and Eugene—thought otherwise on these matters.

"I mean to be great and rich, Mademoiselle," he added after a pause. "I have risked my life for that purpose half a dozen times."

Mathilde stood looking across the room towards the window. He could only see her profile and the straight line of her lips. She too was the product of a generation in which men rose to dazzling heights without the aid of women.

"I should not have troubled you with these details, Mademoiselle," he said, watching her. His instinct was very keen, for not one woman in a thousand, even in those days, would have admitted that love was a detail. "I should not have mentioned it—had you not given me your views—so strangely in harmony with my own."

Whatever his nationality, his voice was that of a Pole—rich, musical, and expressive. He could have made, one would have thought, a very different sort of love had he wished, or had he been sincere. But he was an opportunist. This was the sort of love that Mathilde wanted.

He came a step nearer to her and stood resting on his sword—a lean hard man who had seen much war.

"Until you opened my eyes," he said, "I did not know, or did not care to know, that love, far from being a drag on ambition, may be a help."

Mathilde made a little movement towards him which she instantly repressed. The heart is quicker, but the head nearly always has the last word.

"Mademoiselle," he said—and no doubt he saw the movement and the restraint—"will you help me now at the beginning of the war, and listen to me again at the end of it—if I succeed?"

After all, he was modest in his demands.

"Will you help me? Together, Mademoiselle—to what height may we not rise in these days?"

There was a ring of sincerity in his voice, and her eyes answered it.

"How can I help you?" she asked in a doubting voice.

"Oh, it is a small matter," was the reply. "But it is one in which the Emperor is personally interested. Such things have a special attraction for him. The human interest never fails to hold his attention. If I do well, he will know it and remember me. It is a question, Mademoiselle, of secret societies. You know that Prussia is riddled with them."

Mathilde did not answer. He studied her face, which was clean cut and hard like a marble bust—a good face to hide a secret.

"It is my duty to watch here in Dantzig and to report to the Emperor. In serving myself I could also perhaps serve a friend, one who might otherwise run into danger—who may be in danger while you and I stand here. For the Emperor strikes hard and quickly. I speak of your father, Mademoiselle—and of the Tugendbund."

Still he could not see from the pale profile whether Mathilde knew anything at all.

"And if I procure information for you?" asked she at length, in a quiet and collected voice.

"You will help me to attain a position such as I could ask—even you—to share with me. And you would do your father no harm. You would even render him a service. For all the secret societies in Germany will not stop Napoleon. It is only God who can stop him now, Mademoiselle. All men who attempt it will only be crushed beneath the wheels. I might save your father."

But Mathilde did not seem to be thinking of her father.

"I am hampered by poverty," de Casimir said, changing his ground. "In the old days it did not matter. But now, in the Empire, one must be rich. I shall be rich—at the end of this campaign."

Again his voice was sincere, and again her eyes responded. He made a step forward, and gently taking her hand, he raised it to his lips.

"You will help me!" he said, and, turning abruptly on his heel, he left her.

De Casimir's quarters were in the Langenmarkt. On returning to them, he took from his despatch-case a letter which he turned over thoughtfully in his hand. It was addressed to Désirée, and sealed carefully with a wafer.

"She may as well have it," he said. "It will be as well that she should be occupied with her own affairs."

CHAPTER VIII.

A VISITATION.

Be wiser than other people if you can, but do not tell them so.

WHENEVER Papa Barlasch caught sight of his unwilling host's face, he turned his own aside with a despairing upward nod. Once or twice, during the early days of his occupation of the room behind the kitchen in the Frauengasse, he smote himself sharply on the brow, as if calling upon his brain to make an effort. But afterwards he seemed to resign himself to this lapse of memory, and the upward despairing nod gradually lost intensity until at last he brought himself to pass Antoine Sebastian in the narrow passage with no more emphatic notice than a scowl.

"You and I," he said to Désirée, "are the friends. The others——"

And his gesture seemed to permit the others to go hang if they so desired. The army had gone forward, leaving Dantzig in that idle restlessness which holds those who, finding themselves in a house of sickness, are not permitted entry to the darkened chamber, but must await the crisis elsewhere.

There were some busy enough in the commerce that must exist between a huge army and its base, in the forwarding of war material and stores, in accommodating the sick and sending out in return those who were to fill the gaps. But the Dantzigers themselves had nothing to do. Their prosperous trade was paralyzed. Those who had aught to sell had sold it. The high-seas and the high-roads were alike blocked by the French. And rumour, ever busy among those that wait, ran to and fro in the town.

The Emperor of Russia had been taken prisoner. Napoleon had been checked at the passage of the Niemen. There had been a great battle at Gumbinnen, and the French were in full retreat. Vilna had capitulated to Murat, and the war was at an end. A hundred authentic despatches of the morning were the subject of contemptuous laughter at the supper-table.

Lisa heard these tales in the market-place, and told Désirée, who, as often as not, translated them to Barlasch. But he only held up his wrinkled forefinger and shook it slowly from side to side.

"Woman's chatter!" he said. "What is the German for 'magpie'?"

And on being told the word, he repeated it gravely

to Lisa. For he had not only fulfilled his promise of settling down in the house, but had assumed therein a distinct and clearly defined position. He was the counsellor, and from his chair just within the kitchen he gave forth judgment.

"And you," he said to Désirée one morning, when household affairs had taken her to the kitchen, "you are troubled this morning. You have had a letter from your husband?"

"Yes—and he is in good health."

"Ah!"

Barlasch glared at her beneath his brows, looking her up and down, noting her quick movements, which had the uncertainty of youth.

"And now that he is gone," he said, "and that there is war, you are going to employ yourself by falling in love with him, when you had all the time before, and did not take advantage of it."

Désirée laughed at him and made no other answer. While she spoke to Lisa he sat and watched them.

"It would be like a woman to do such a thing," he pursued. "They are so inconvenient—women. They get married for fun, and then one fine Thursday they find they have missed all the fun, like one who comes late to the theatre—when the music is over."

He went to the table and examined the morning marketing, which Lisa had laid out in preparation for dinner. Of some of her purchases he approved, but he laughed aloud at a lettuce which had no heart, and at such a buyer.

Then Désirée attracted his scrutiny again.

"Yes," he said, half to himself, "I see it. You are in love. Just Heaven, I know! I have had them in love with me. . . . Barlasch."

"That must have been a long time ago," answered Désirée with her gay laugh, only giving him half her attention.

"Yes, it was a century ago. But they were the same then as they are now, as they always will be —inconvenient. They waited, however, till they were grown up!"

And with his ever-ready accusing finger he drew Désirée's attention to her own slimness. They were left alone for a minute while Lisa answered a knock at the door, during which time Barlasch sat in grim silence.

"It is a letter," said Lisa, returning. "A sailor brought it."

"Another?" said Barlasch, with a gesture of despair.

"Can you give me news of Charles?" Désirée read, in a writing that was unknown to her. "I shall wait a reply until midnight on board the *Elsa*, lying off the Krahn-Thor." The letter bore the signature,

"Louis d'Arragon." Désirée turned slowly and went upstairs, carrying it folded small in her closed hand.

She was alone in the house, for Mathilde was out and her father had not yet returned from his evening walk. She stood at the head of the stairs, where the last of the daylight filtered through the barred window, and read the letter again. Then she turned and gave a slight start to see Barlasch at the foot of the stairs beckoning to her. He made no attempt to come up, but stood on the mat like a dog that has been forbidden the upper rooms.

"Is it about your father?" he asked, in a hoarse whisper.

"No!"

He made a gesture commanding secrecy and silence. Then he went to close the kitchen door and returned on tip-toe.

"It is," he explained, "that they are talking of him in the cafés. There are many to be arrested to-morrow. They say the patron is one of them, and employs himself in plotting. That his name is not Sebastian at all. That he is a Frenchman who escaped the guillotine. What do I know? It is the gossip of the cafés. But I tell it you because we are friends, you and I. And some day I may want you to do something for me. One thinks of one's self, eh? It is good to make friends. For some day one may want them. That is why I do it. I think of myself. An old soldier. Of the Guard."

With many gestures of tremendous import, and a face all wrinkled and twisted with mystery, he returned to the kitchen.

Mathilde was not to return until late. She had gone to the house of the old Gräfin whose reminiscences had been a fruitful topic at Désirée's wedding. After dining there she and the Gräfin were to go together to a farewell reception given by the Governor. For Rapp was bound for the frontier with the rest, and was to go to the war as first aide-de-camp to the Emperor.

Mathilde could not be back until ten o'clock. She, who was so quick and quiet, had been much occupied in social observances lately, and had made fast friends with the Gräfin during the last few days, constantly going to see her.

Désirée knew that what Barlasch had repeated as the gossip of the cafés was in part, if not wholly, true. She and Mathilde had long known that any mention of France had the instant effect of turning their father into a man of stone. It was the skeleton in this quiet house that sat at table with its inmates, a shadowy fourth tying their tongues. The rattle of its bones seemed to paralyze Sebastian's mind, and at any moment he would fall into a dumb and stricken apathy which terrified those about him. At such times it seemed that one thought in his mind had swallowed all the rest, so that he heard without understanding and saw without perceiving.

He was in such a humour when he came back to dinner. He passed Désirée on the stairs without speaking and went to his room to change his clothes, for he never relaxed his formal habits. At the dinner-table he glanced at her as a dog, knowing that he is ill, may be seen to glance with a secret air at his master, wondering whether he is detected.

Désirée had always hoped that her father would speak to her when this humour was upon him and tell her the meaning of it. Perhaps it would come to-night, when they were alone. There was an un-spoken sympathy existing between them in which Mathilde took no share, which had even shut out Charles as out of a room where there was no light, into which Désirée and her father went at times and stood hand-in-hand without speaking.

They dined in silence, while Lisa hurried about her duties, oppressed by a sense of unknown fear. After dinner they went to the drawing-room as usual. It had been a dull day, with great clouds creeping up from the West. The evening fell early, and the lamps were already alight. Désirée looked to the wicks with the eye of experience when she entered the room. Then she went to the window. Lisa did not always draw the curtains effectually. She glanced down into the street, and turned suddenly on her heel, facing her father.

"They are there," she said. For she had seen shadowy forms lurking beneath the trees of the Frauengasse. The street was ill-lighted, but she knew the shadows of the trees.

"How many?" asked Sebastian, in a dull voice.

She glanced at him quickly—at his still, frozen face and quiescent hands. He was not going to rise to the occasion, as he sometimes did even from his deepest apathy. She must do alone anything that was to be accomplished to-night.

The house, like many in the Frauengasse, had been built by a careful Hanseatic merchant, whose warehouse was his own cellar half sunk beneath the level of the street. The door of the warehouse was immediately under the front door, down a few steps below the street, while a few more steps, broad and footworn, led up to the stone veranda and the level of the lower dwelling-rooms. A guard placed in the street could thus watch both doors without moving.

There was a third door, giving exit from the little room where Barlasch slept to the small yard where he had placed those trunks which were made in France.

Désirée had no time to think. She came of a race

of women of a brighter intelligence than any women in the world. She took her father by the arm and hastened downstairs. Barlasch was at his post within the kitchen door. His eyes shone suddenly as he saw her face. It was said of Papa Barlasch that he was a gay man in battle, laughing and making a hundred jests, but at other times lugubrious. Désirée saw him smile for the first time, in the dim light of the passage.

"They are there in the street," he said, "I have seen them. I thought you would come to Barlasch. They all do—the women. In here. Leave him to me. When they ring the bell, receive them yourself—with smiles. They are only men. Let them search the house if they want to. Tell them he has gone to the reception with Mademoiselle."

As he spoke the bell rang just above his head. He looked up at it and laughed.

"Ah, ah!" he said, "the fanfare begins."

He drew Sebastian within and closed the door of his little room. Lisa had already gone to answer the bell. When she opened the door three men stepped quickly over the threshold, and one of them, thrusting her aside, closed the door and turned the key. Désirée, in her white evening dress, on the bottom step, just beneath the lamp that hung from the ceiling, made them pause and look at each other. Then one of the three came towards her, hat in hand.

"Our duty, Fräulein," he said awkwardly. "We are but obeying orders. A mere formality. It will all be explained, no doubt, if the householder, Antoine Sebastian, will put on his hat and come with us."

"His hat is not there, as you see," answered Désirée. "You must seek him elsewhere."

The man shook his head with a knowing smile. "We must seek him in this house," he said. "We will make it as easy for you as we can, Fräulein—if you make it easy for us."

As he spoke he produced a candle from his pocket, and encouraged the broken wick with his finger-nail.

"It will make it pleasanter for all," said Désirée cheerfully, "if you will accept a candlestick."

The man glanced at her. He was a heavy man, with little suspicious eyes set close together. He seemed to be concluding that she had outwitted him —that Sebastian was not in the house.

"Where are the cellar-stairs?" he asked. "I warn you, Fräulein, it is useless to conceal your father. We shall, of course, find him."

Désirée pointed to the door next to that giving entry to the kitchen. It was bolted and locked. Désirée found the key for them. She not only gave them every facility, but was anxious that they should be as quick as possible. They did not linger in the cellar, which, though vast, was empty; and when they returned Désirée, who was waiting for them, led the way upstairs.

They were rather abashed by her silence. They would have preferred protestations and argument. Discussion always belittles. The smile recommended by Papa Barlasch, lurking at the corner of her lips, made them feel foolish. She was so slight and young . and helpless, that a sort of shame rendered them clumsy.

They felt more at home in the kitchen when they arrived there, and the sight of Lisa, sturdy and defiant, reminded them of the authority upon which Désirée had somehow cast a mystic contempt.

"There is a door there," said the heavy official, with a brusque return of his early manner. "Come, what is that door?"

"That is a little room."

"Then open it."

"I cannot," returned Lisa. "It is locked."

"Aha!" said the man, with a laugh of much meaning. "On the inside, eh?"

He went to it, and banged on it with his fist.

"Come," he shouted, "open it and be done."

There was a short silence, during which those in the kitchen listened breathlessly. A shuffling sound inside the door made the officer of the law turn and beckon to his two men to come closer.

Then, after some fumbling, as of one in the dark, the door was unlocked and slowly opened.

Papa Barlasch stood in a very primitive night-apparel within the door. He had not done things by halves, for he was an old campaigner, and knew that a thing half done is better left undone in times of war. He noted the presence of Désirée and Lisa, but was not ashamed. The reason of it was soon apparent. For Papa Barlasch was drunk, and the smell of drink came out of his apartment in a warm wave.

"It is the soldier billeted in the house," explained Lisa, with a half-hysterical laugh.

Then Barlasch harangued them in the language of intoxication. If he had not spared Désirée's feelings, he spared her ears less now; for he was an ignorant man, who had lived through a brutal period in the world's history the roughest life a man can lead. Two of the men held him with difficulty against the wall, while the third hastily searched the room—where, indeed, no one could well be concealed.

Then they quitted the house, followed by the polyglot curses of Barlasch, who was now endeavouring to find his bayonet amidst his chaotic possessions.

CHAPTER IX.

THE GOLDEN GUESS.

The golden guess
Is morning star to the full round of truth.

BARLASCH was never more sober in his life than when
he emerged a minute later from his room, while Lisa
was still feverishly bolting the door. He had not
wasted much time at his toilet. In his flannel shirt,
his arms bare to the elbow, knotted and muscular,
he looked like some rude son of toil.

"One thinks of one's self," he hastened to explain
to Désirée, fearing that she might ascribe some other
motive to his action. "Some day the patron may be
in power again, and then he will remember a poor
soldier. It is good to think of the future."

He shook his head pessimistically at Lisa as
belonging to a sex liable to error: instanced in this
case by bolting the door too eagerly.

"Now," he said, turning to Désirée again, "have
you any in Dantzig to help you?"

"Yes," she answered rather slowly.

H

"Then send for him."

"I cannot do that."

"Then go for him yourself," snapped Barlasch impatiently.

He looked at her fiercely beneath his shaggy eyebrows.

"It is no use to be afraid," he said; "you are afraid —I see it in your face. And it is never any use. Before they hammered on that door there, my legs shook. For I am easily afraid—I. But it is never any use. And when one opens the door, it goes."

He looked at her with a puzzled frown, seeking in vain, it may have been, the ordinary symptoms of fear. She was hesitating but not afraid. There ran blood in her veins which will for all time be associated by history with a gay and indomitable courage.

"Come," he said sharply; "there is nothing else to do."

"I will go," said Désirée, at length, deciding suddenly to do the one thing that is left to a woman once or twice in her life—to go to the one man and trust him.

"By the back way," said Barlasch, helping her with the cloak that Lisa had brought, and pulling the hood forward over her face with a jerk. "Ah, I know that way. The patron is hiding in the yard. An old soldier looks to the retreat—though the Emperor has saved us that, so far. Come, I will help you over the wall, for the door is rusted."

The way, which Barlasch had perceived, led through the room at the back of the kitchen to a yard, and thence through a door not opened by the present occupiers of the old house, into a very labyrinth of narrow alleys running downward to the river and round the tall houses that stand against the cathedral walls.

The wall was taller than Barlasch, but he ran at it like a cat, and Désirée standing below could see the black outline of his limbs crouching on the top. He stooped down, and grasping her hands, lifted her by the sheer strength of one arm, balanced her for an instant on the wall, and then lowered her on the outer side.

"Run," he whispered.

She knew the way, and although the night was dark, and these narrow alleys between high walls had no lamps, Désirée lost no time. The Krahn-Thor is quite near to the Frauengasse. Indeed, the whole of Dantzig occupied but a small space between the rivers in those straitened days. The town was quieter than it had been for months, and Désirée passed unmolested through the narrow streets. She made her way to the quay, passing through the low gateway known as the door of the Holy Ghost, and here found people still astir. For the commerce that thrives on a northern river is paralyzed all the winter, and feverishly active when the ice has gone.

"The *Elsa*," replied a woman, who had been selling bread all day on the quay, and was now packing up her stall, "you ask for the *Elsa*. There is such a ship, I know. But how can I say which she is? See, they lie right across the river like a bridge. Besides, it is late, and sailors are rough men."

Désirée hurried on. Louis d'Arragon had said that the ship was lying near to the Krahn-Thor, of which the great hooded roof loomed darkly against the stars above her. She was looking about her when a man came forward with the hesitating step of one who has been told to wait the arrival of some one unknown to him.

"The *Elsa*," she said to him; "which ship is it?"

"Come along with me, Mademoiselle," the man replied; "though I was not told to look for a woman."

He spoke in English, which Désirée hardly understood; for she had never heard it from English lips, and looked for the first time on one of that race upon which all the world waited now for salvation. For the English, of all the nations, were the only men who from the first had consistently defied Napoleon.

The sailor led the way towards the river. As he passed the lamp burning dimly above some steps,

Désirée saw that he was little more than a boy. He turned and offered her his hand with a shy laugh, and together they stood at the bottom of the steps with the water lapping at their feet.

"Have you a letter," he said, "or will you come on board?"

Then perceiving that she did not understand, he repeated the question in German.

"I will come on board," she answered.

"The *Elsa* was lying in the middle of the river, and the boat into which Désirée stepped shot across the water without sound of oars. The sailor was paddling it noiselessly at the stern. Désirée was not unused to boats, and when they came alongside the *Elsa* she climbed on board without help.

"This way," said the sailor, leading her towards the deckhouse where a light burned dimly behind red curtains. He knocked at the door and opened it without awaiting a reply. In the little cabin two men sat at a table, and one of them was Louis d'Arragon dressed in the rough clothes of a merchant seaman. He seemed to recognize Désirée at once, though she still stood without the door, in the darkness.

"You?" he said in surprise. "I did not expect you, madame. You want me?"

"Yes," answered Désirée, stepping over the combing. Louis's companion, who was also a sailor, coarsely clad, rose and, awkwardly taking off his cap, hurried to the door, murmuring some vague apology. It is not always the roughest men who have the worst manners towards women.

He closed the door behind him, leaving Désirée and Louis looking at each other by the light of an oil lamp that flickered and gave forth a greasy smell. The little cabin was smoke-ridden, and smelt of ancient tar. It was no bigger than the table in the drawing-room in the Frauengasse, across which he had bowed to her in farewell a few days earlier, little knowing when and where they were to meet again. For fate can always turn a surprise better than the human fancy.

Behind the curtain, the window stood open, and the high, clear song of the wind through the rigging filled the little cabin with a continuous minor note of warning which must have been part of his life; for he must have heard it, as all sailors do, sleeping or waking, night and day.

He was probably so accustomed to it that he never heeded it. But it filled Désirée's ears, and whenever she heard it in after-life, in memory this moment came again to her, and she looked back to it, as a traveller may look back to a milestone at a cross-road, and wonder where his journey might have ended had he taken another turning.

"My father," she said quickly, "is in danger. There is no one else in Dantzig to whom we can turn, and——"

She paused. What was she going to add? She hesitated, and then was silent. There was no reason why she should have elected to come to him. At all events she gave none.

"I am glad I was in Dantzig when it happened," he said, turning to take up his cap, which was of rough dark fur, such as seamen wear even in summer at night in the Northern seas.

"Come," he added, "you can tell me as we go ashore."

But they did not speak while the sailor sculled the boat to the steps. On the quay they would probably pass unnoticed, for there were many strange sailors at this time in Dantzig, and Louis d'Arragon might easily be mistaken for one of the French seamen who had brought stores by sea from Bordeaux and Brest and Cherbourg.

"Now tell me," he said, as they walked side by side; and in voluble French, Désirée launched into her story. It was rather incoherent, by reason, perhaps, of its frankness.

"Stop—stop," he interrupted gravely, "who is Barlasch?"

Louis walked rather slowly in his stiff sea-boots at

her side, and she instinctively spoke less rapidly as she explained the part that Barlasch had played.

"And you trust him?"

"Of course," she answered.

"But why?"

"Oh, you are so matter-of-fact," she exclaimed; "I do not know. Because he is trustworthy, I suppose."

She continued the story, but suddenly stopped and looked up at him under the shadow of her hood.

"You are silent," she said. "Do you know something about my father of which I am ignorant? Is that it?"

"No," he answered, "I am trying to follow—that is all. You leave so much to my imagination."

"But I have no time to explain things," she protested. "Every moment is of value. I will explain all those things some other time. At this moment all I can think of is my father and the danger he is in. If it had not been for Barlasch, he would have been in prison by now. And as it is, the danger is only half averted. For he, himself, is so little help. All must be done for him. He will do nothing for himself while this humour is upon him; you understand?"

"Partly," he answered slowly.

"Oh!" she exclaimed half-impatiently, "one sees that you are an Englishman."

And she found time, even in her hurry, to laugh. For she was young enough to float buoyant upon that sea of hope which ebbs in the course of years and leaves men stranded on the hard facts of life.

"You forget," he said in self-defence.

"I forget what?"

"That a week ago I had never seen Dantzig, or your father, or your sister, or the Frauengasse. A week ago I did not know that there was anybody called Sebastian in the world—and did not care."

"Yes," she admitted thoughtfully, "I had forgotten that."

And they walked on in silence, a long way, till they came to the Gate of the Holy Ghost.

"But you can help him to escape?" she said at length, as if following the course of her own thoughts.

"Yes," he answered, and that was all.

They passed through the smaller streets in silence, and Désirée led the way into a narrow alley running between the street of the Holy Ghost and the Frauengasse.

"There is the wall to be climbed," she said; but, as she spoke, the door giving exit to the alley was cautiously opened by Barlasch.

"A little oil," he whispered, "and it was soon done."

The yard was dark within, for there might be watchers at any of the windows above them in the pointed gables that made patterns against the star-lit sky.

"All is well," said Barlasch; "those sons of dogs have not returned, and the patron is waiting in the kitchen, cloaked and ready for a journey. He has collected himself—the patron."

He led the way through his own room, which was dark, save for a shaft of lamp-light coming from the kitchen. He looked back keenly at Louis d'Arragon.

"Salut!" he growled, scowling at his boots. "A sailor," he muttered after a pause. "Good. She has her wits at the top of the basket—that child."

Désirée was throwing back her hood and looking at her father with a reassuring smile.

"I have brought Monsieur d'Arragon," she said, "to help us."

For Sebastian has not recognized the new-comer. He now bowed in his stiff way, and began a formal apology, which D'Arragon cut short with a quick gesture.

"It is the least I could do," he said, "in the absence of Charles. Have you money?"

"Yes—a little."

"You will require money and a few clothes. I can get you a passage to Riga or to Helsingborg to-night. From there you can communicate with your daughter.

Events will follow each other rapidly. One never knows what a week may bring forth in time of war. It may be safe for you to return soon. Come, monsieur, we must go."

Sebastian made a gesture with his outspread arms, half of protestation, half of acquiescence. It was plain that he had no sympathy with these modern, hurried methods of meeting the emergencies of daily life. A valise, packed and strapped, lay on the table. D'Arragon weighed it in his hand, and then lifted it to his shoulder.

"Come, monsieur," he repeated leading the way through Barlasch's room to the yard. "And you," he added, addressing himself to that soldier, "shut the door behind us."

With another gesture of protest Sebastian gathered his cloak round him and followed. D'Arragon had taken Désirée so literally at her word that he allowed her father no time for hesitation, nor a moment to say farewell.

She was alone in the kitchen before she had realized that they were going. In a minute Barlasch returned. She could hear him setting in order the room which had been hurriedly disorganized in order to open the door leading to the yard, where her father had concealed himself. He was muttering to himself as he lifted the furniture.

Coming back into the kitchen, he found Désirée standing where he had left her. Glancing at her, he scratched his grey head in a plebeian way, and gave a little laugh.

"Yes," he said, pointing to the spot where D'Arragon had stood. "That was a man, that you fetched to help us—a man. It makes a difference when such as that goes out of the room—eh?"

He busied himself in the kitchen, setting in order that which remained of the *mise en scène* of his violent reception of the secret police. Suddenly he turned in his emphatic manner, and threw out his rugged forefinger to hold her attention.

"If there had been some like that in Paris, there would have been no Revolution. Za-za, za-za!" he concluded, imitating effectively the buzz of many voices in an assembly. "Words and not deeds," Barlasch protested. Whereas to-night, he clearly showed by two gestures, they had met a man of deeds.

CHAPTER X.

IN DEEP WATER.

Le cœur humain est un abîme qui trompe tous les calculs.

IT is to be presumed that Colonel de Casimir met friends at the reception given by Governor Rapp in the great rooms of the Rathhaus. For there were many Poles present, and not a few officers of other nationalities.

The army indeed that set forth to conquer Russia was not a French-speaking army. Less than half of the regiments were of that nationality, while Italians, Bavarians, Saxons, Wurtembergers, Westphalians, Prussians, Swiss, and Portuguese went gaily forward on the great venture. There were soldiers from the numerous petty states of the German Confederation which acknowledged Napoleon as their protector, for the good reason that they could not protect themselves against him. Finally, there were those Poles who had fought in Spain for Napoleon, hoping that in return he would some day set the ancient kingdom upon its feet among the nations. Already the whisperers pointed to Davoust as the future king of the new Poland.

Many present at the farewell reception of the Governor carried a sword, though they were the merest civilians, plotting, counter-plotting, and whispering a hundred rumours. Perhaps Rapp himself, speaking bluff French with a German accent, was as honest as any man in the room, though he lacked the polish of the Parisian and had not the subtlety of the Pole. Rapp was not a shining light in these brilliant circles. He was a Governor not for peace, but for war. His day was yet to come.

Such men as de Casimir shrugged their supple shoulders at his simple talk. They spoke of him half-contemptuously as of one who had had a thousand chances and had never taken them. He was not even rich, and he had handled great sums of money. He was only a General, and he had slept in the Emperor's tent—had had access to him in every humour. He might do the same again in the coming campaign. He was worth cultivating. De Casimir and his like were full of smiles which in no wise deceived the shrewd Alsatian.

Mathilde Sebastian was among the ladies to whom these brilliant warriors paid their uncouth compliments. Perhaps de Casimir was aware that her measuring eyes followed him wherever he went. He knew, at all events, that he could hold his own amid these adventurers, many of whom had risen from the ranks; while others, from remote northern States, had birth but no manners at all.. He was easy and gay, carrying lightly that subtle air of distinction which is vouchsafed to many Poles.

"Here to-day, Mademoiselle, and gone to-morrow," he said. "All these eager soldiers. And who can tell which of us may return?"

If he had expected Mathilde to flinch at this reminder of his calling, he was disappointed. Her eyes were hard and bright. She had had so few chances of moving amidst this splendour, of seeing close at hand the greatness which Napoleon shed around him as the sun its rays. She was carried away by the spirit of the age. Anything was better, she felt, than obscurity.

"And who can tell," whispered de Casimir with a careless and confident laugh, "which of us shall come back rich and great?"

This brought the glance from her dark eyes for which his own lay waiting. She was certainly beautiful, and wore the difficult dress of that day with assurance and grace. She possessed something which the German ladies about her lacked; something which many suddenly lack when a Frenchwoman is near.

His manner, half respectful, half triumphant, betrayed an understanding to which he did not refer in words. She had bestowed some favour upon him—had acceded to some request He hoped for more. He had overstepped some barrier. She, who should have measured the distance, had allowed him to come too close. The barriers of love are one-sided; there is no climbing back.

"A hundred envious eyes are watching me," he said in an undertone as he passed on; "I dare not stay longer. I am on duty to-night."

She bowed and watched him go. She was, it would seem, aware of that fallen barrier. She had done nothing, had permitted nothing from weakness. There was no weakness at all perhaps in Mathilde Sebastian. She had the quiet manner of a skilled card-player with folded cards laid face down upon the table, who knows what is in her hand and is waiting for the foe to lead.

De Casimir did not see her again. In such a throng it would have been difficult to find her had he so desired. But, as he had told her, he was on duty to-night. There were to be a hundred arrests before dawn. Many who were laughing and talking with the French officers to-night were already in the grasp of Napoleon's secret police, and would drive straight from the door of the Rathhaus to the town prison or to the old Watch-house in the Portchaisen-gasse. Others, moving through the great rooms with a high head, were already condemned out of their own bureaux and escritoires now being rifled by the Emperor's spies.

The Emperor himself had given the order, before quitting Dantzig to take command of the maddest and greatest enterprise conceived by the mind of man. There was nothing above the reach of his mind, it seemed, and nothing too low for him to bend down and touch. Every detail had been considered by himself. He was like a man who, having an open wound on his back, attends to it hurriedly before showing an undaunted face to the enemy.

His inexorable finger had come down on the name of Antoine Sebastian, figuring on all the secret reports —first in many.

"Who is this man?" he asked, and none could answer.

He had gone to the frontier without awaiting the solution to the question. Such was his method now. He had so much to do that he could but skim the surface of his task. For the human mind, though it be colossal, can only work within certain limits. The greatest orator in the world can only move his immediate hearers. Those beyond the inner circle catch a word here and there, and imagination supplies the rest or improves upon it. But those in the farthest gallery hear nothing and see a little man gesticulating.

De Casimir was not entrusted with the execution of the Emperor's orders. As a member of General Rapp's staff, resident in Dantzig since the city's occupation by the French, he had been called upon to make exhaustive reports upon the feeling of the burghers. There were many doubtful cases. De Casimir did not pretend to be better than his fellows. To some he had sold the benefit of the doubt. Some had paid willingly enough for their warning. Others had put off the payment; for there were many Jews, then as now, in Dantzig; slow payers requiring something stronger than a threat to make them disburse.

De Casimir therefore quitted the Rathhaus among the first to go, and walked through the busy streets to his rooms in the Langenmarkt, where he not only lived but had a small office to which orderlies and aides-de-camp came by day or night. Two sentries kept guard on the pavement. Since the spring, this office had been one of the busiest military posts in Dantzig. Its doors were open at all hours, and in truth many of de Casimir's assistants preferred to transact their business in the dark.

There might be some recalcitrant debtor driven by stress of circumstance to clear his conscience to-night. It would be as well, de Casimir thought, to be at one's post. Nor was he mistaken. Though it was only ten o'clock, two men were awaiting his return, and, their business despatched, de Casimir deemed it wise to send away his assistants. Immediately after they had gone a woman came. She was half distracted with fear, and the tears ran down her pallid cheeks. But she dried them at the mention of de Casimir's price, and fell to abusing him.

"If your husband is innocent, there is all the more reason why he should be grateful to me for warning him," he said, with a smile. And at last the lady paid and went away.

The town clocks had struck eleven before another footstep on the pavement made de Casimir raise his head. He did not actually expect any one, but a certain surreptitiousness in the approach of this visitor, and the low knock on the door, made him suspect that this was grist for his mill.

He opened the door and, seeing that it was a woman, stepped back. When she had entered, he closed the door while she stood watching him in the dark passage, beneath the shadow of her hood. Knowing the value of such small details, he locked the door rather ostentatiously and dropped the key into his pocket.

"And now, madame," he said reassuringly, as he

followed his visitor into the room where a shaded lamp lighted his writing-table. She threw back her hood, and it was Mathilde! The surprise on de Casimir's face was genuine enough. Romance could not have brought about this visit, nor love be its motive.

"Something has happened," he said, looking at her doubtfully.

"Where is my father?" was the reply.

"Unless there has been some mistake," he answered glibly, "he is at home in bed."

She smiled contemptuously into his innocent face.

"There has been a mistake," she said, "they came to arrest him to-night."

De Casimir made a gesture of anger and seemed to be mentally assigning a punishment to some blunderer.

"And?" he asked, without looking at her.

"And he escaped."

"For the moment?"

"No; he has left Dantzig."

Something in her voice—the cold note of warning —made him glance uneasily at her. This was not a woman to be deceived, and yet she was womanly enough to fear deception and to resent her own fears, visiting her anger on any who aroused them. In the flash of an eye he understood her, and forestalled the words that were upon her lips.

"And I promised that he should come to no harm—I know that," he said quickly. "At first I thought that it must have been a blunder, but on reflection I am sure that it is not. It is the Emperor. He must have given the order for the arrest himself, behind my back. That is his way. He trusts no one. He deceives those nearest to him. I made out the list of those to be arrested to-night, and your father's name was not on it. Do you believe me? Mademoiselle, do you believe me?"

It was only natural in such a man to look for disbelief. The air he breathed was infected by suspicion. No deception was too small for the great man whom he served. Mathilde made no answer.

"You came here to accuse me of having deceived you," he said rather anxiously. "Is that it?"

She nodded without meeting his eyes. It was not the truth. She had come to hear his defence, hoping against hope that she might be able to believe him.

"Mathilde," he asked slowly, "do you believe me?"

He came a step nearer, looking down at her averted face, which was oddly white. Then suddenly she turned, without a sound, without lifting her eyes—and was in his arms. It seemed that she had done it against her will, and it took him by surprise. He had thought that she was trying to attract his love because she believed in his capability to make his fortune like so many soldiers of France; that she was only playing a woman's subtle game. And, after all, she was like the rest—a little cleverer, a little colder —but, like the rest.

While his arms were still round her, his quick mind leapt forward to the future, wondering already to what end this would lead them. For a moment he was taken aback. He was over the last of those barriers which are so easy from the outside and un-climbable from within. She had thrust into his hands a power greater than, for the moment, he knew how to wield. It was characteristic of him to think first whither it would lead him, and next how he could turn it to good account.

Some instinct told him that this was a different love from any that he had met before. The same instinct made him understand that it was crying aloud to be convinced; and, oddly enough, he had told her the truth.

"See," he said, "here is a copy of the list, and your father's name is not on it. See, here is Napoleon's letter, expressing satisfaction with my work here and in Königsberg, where I have been served by an agent of my own choosing. Many have climbed to a throne with less than that letter for their first step. See . . . !" he opened another drawer. It was full of money.

"See, again!" he said with a low laugh, and from an iron chest he took two or three bags which fell upon the table with the discreet unmistakable chink of gold. "That is the Emperor's. He trusts me, you see. These bags are mine. They are to be sent back to France before I follow the army to Russia. What I have told you is true, you see."

It was an odd way of wooing, but this man rarely made a mistake. There are many women who, like Mathilde Sebastian, are readier to love success than console failure.

"See," he said, after a moment's hesitation, opening another drawer in his writing-table, "before I went away I had intended to ask you to remember me."

As he spoke he drew a jewel case from under some papers, and slowly opened it. He had others like it in the drawer; for emergencies.

"But I never hoped," he went on, "to have an opportunity of seeing you thus alone—to ask you never to forget me. You permit me?"

He clasped the diamonds round her throat, and they glittered on the poor, cheap dress, which was the best she had. She looked down at them with a catching breath, and for an instant the glitter was reflected in her eyes.

She had come asking for reassurance, and he gave her diamonds; which is an old tale told over and over again. For in human love we have to accept not what we want, but what is given to us.

"No one in Dantzig," he said, "is so glad to hear that your father has escaped as I am."

And, with the glitter still lurking in her dark-grey eyes, she believed him. He drew her cloak round her, and gently brought her hood over her hair.

"I must take you home," he said tenderly, "without delay. And as we go through the streets you must tell me how it happened, and how you were able to come to me."

"Désirée was not asleep," she answered; "she was waiting for me to return, and told me at once. Then she went to bed, and I waited until she was asleep. It was she who managed the escape."

De Casimir, who was locking the drawers of his writing-table, glanced up sharply.

"Ah! but not alone?"

"No—not alone. I will tell you as we go through the streets."

CHAPTER XI.

THE WAVE MOVES ON.

La même fermeté qui sert à résister à l'amour sert aussi à le rendre violent et durable.

IT is only in war that the unexpected admittedly happens. In love and other domestic calamities there is always a relative who knew it all the time.

The news that Napoleon was in Vilna, hastily evacuated by the Russians in full retreat, came as a surprise and not to all as a pleasant one, in Dantzig.

It was Papa Barlasch who brought the tidings to the Frauengasse, one hot afternoon in July. He returned before his usual hour, and sent Lisa upstairs, with a message given in dumb show and interpreted by her into matter-of-fact German, that he must see the young ladies without delay. Far back in the great days of the monarchy, Papa Barlasch must have been a little child in a peasant's hut on those Côtes du Nord where they breed a race of Frenchmen startlingly similar to the hereditary foe across the Channel, where to this day the men kick off their sabots at the door, and hold that an honest labourer has no business under a roof except in stocking-feet and shirt-sleeves.

Barlasch had never yet been upstairs in the Sebastians' house, and deemed it only respectful to the ladies to take off his boots on the mat, and prowl to the kitchen in coarse blue woollen stockings, carefully darned by himself, under the scornful immediate eye of Lisa.

He was in the kitchen when Mathilde and Désirée, in obedience to his command, came downstairs. The floor in one corner of the room was littered with his belongings; for he never used the table. "He takes up no more room than a cat," Lisa once said of him. "I never fall over him."

"She leaves her greasy plates here and there," explained Barlasch in return. "One must think of one's self and one's uniform."

He was in his stocking-feet with unbuttoned tunic when the two girls came to him.

"Aï, aï, aï," he said, imitating with his two hands the galloping of a horse. "The Russians," he explained confidentially.

"Has there been a battle?" asked Désirée.

And Barlasch answered "Pooh!" not without contempt for the female understanding.

"Then what is it?" she inquired. "You must remember we are not soldiers—we do not understand those manœuvres—aï, aï, like that."

And she copied his gesture beneath his scowling contempt.

"It is Vilna," he said. "That is what it is. Then it will be Smolensk, and then Moscow. Ah, ah! That little man!"

He turned and took up his haversack.

"And I—I have my route. It is good-bye to the Frauengasse. We have been friends. I told you we should be. It is good-bye to these ladies—and to that Lisa. Look at her!"

He pointed with his curved and derisive finger into Lisa's eyes. And in truth the tears were there. Lisa was in heart and person that which is comprehensively called motherly. She saw perhaps some pathos in the sight of this rugged man—worn by travel, bent with hardship and many wounds, past his work—shouldering his haversack and trudging off to the war.

"The wave moves on," he said, making a gesture, and a sound illustrating that watery progress. "And Dantzig will soon be forgotten. You will be left in peace—but we go on to—— " He paused and shrugged his shoulders while attending to a strap. "India or the devil," he concluded

"Colonel Casimir has gone," he added in what he took to be an aside to Mathilde. Which made her wonder for a moment. "I saw him depart with his staff soon after daybreak. And the Emperor has forgotten Dantzig. It is safe enough for the patron now. You can write him a letter to tell him so. Tell him that I said it was safe for him to return quietly here, and live in the Frauengasse—I, Barlasch."

He was ready now, and, buttoning his tunic, he fixed the straps across his chest, looking from one to the other of the three women watching him, not without some appreciation of an audience. Then he turned to Désirée, who had always been his friend, with whom he now considered that he had the soldier's bond of a peril passed through together.

"The Emperor has forgotten Dantzig," he repeated, "and those against whom he had a grudge. But he has also forgotten those who are in prison. It is not good to be forgotten in prison. Tell the patron that— to put it in his pipe and smoke it. Some day he may remember an old soldier. Ah, one thinks of one's self."

And beneath his bushy brows he looked at her with a gleam of cunning. He went to the door and, turning there, pointed the finger of scorn at Lisa, stout and tearful. He gave a short laugh of a low-born contempt, and departed without further parley.

On the doorstep he paused to put on his boots and button his gaiters, stooping clumsily with a groan beneath his burden of haversack and kit. Désirée, who had had time to go upstairs to her bedroom, ran after him as he descended the steps. She had her purse in her hand, and she thrust it into his, quickly and breathlessly.

"If you take it," she said.   "I shall know that we are friends."

He took it ungraciously enough. It was a silken thing with two small rings to keep the money in place, and he looked at it with a grimace, weighing it in his hand. It was very light.

"Money," he said. "No, thank you. To get drink with, and be degraded and sent to prison. Not for me, madame. No, thank you. One thinks of one's career."

And with a gruff laugh of worldly wisdom he continued his way down the worn steps, never looking back at her as she stood in the sunlight watching him, with the purse in her hand.

So in his old age Papa Barlasch was borne forward to the war on that human tide which flooded all Lithuania, and never ebbed again, but sank into the barren ground, and was no more seen.

As the slow autumn approached, it became apparent that Dantzig no longer interested the watchers. Vilna became the base of operations. Smolensk fell, and, most wonderful of all, the Russians were retiring on Moscow. Dantzig was no longer on the route. For a time it was of the world forgotten, while, as Barlasch had predicted, free men continued at liberty, though their names had an evil savour, while innocent persons in prison were left to rot there.

Désirée continued to receive letters from her husband, full of love and war. For a long time he lingered at Königsberg, hoping every day to be sent forward. Then he followed Murat across the Niemen, and wrote of weary journeys over the rolling plains of Lithuania.

Towards the end of July he mentioned curtly the arrival of de Casimir at head-quarters.

"With him came a courier," wrote Charles, "bringing your dead letter. I don't believe you love me as I love you. At all events, you do not seem to tell me that you do so often as I want to tell you. Tell me what you do and think every moment of the day. . . ." And so on. Charles seemed to write as easily as he talked, and had no difficulty in setting forth his feelings. "The courier is in the saddle," he concluded. "De Casimir tells me that I must finish. Write and tell me everything. How is Mathilde? And your father? Is he in good health? How does he pass his day? Does he still go out in the evening to his café?"

This seemed to be an afterthought, suggested perhaps by conversation passing in the room in which he sat.

The other exile, writing from Stockholm, was briefer in his communications.

"I am well," wrote Antoine Sebastian, "and hope to arrive soon after you receive this. Felix Meyer, the notary, has instructions to furnish you with money for household expenses."

It would appear that Sebastian possessed other friends in Dantzig, who had kept him advised of all that passed in the city.

For neither Mathilde nor Désirée had obeyed Barlasch's blunt order to write to their father. They did not know whither he had fled, neither had they received any communication giving an address or a hint as to his future movements. It would appear that the same direct and laconic mind which had carried out his escape deemed it wiser that those left behind should be in no position to furnish information.

In fairness to Barlasch, Désirée had made little of that soldier's part in Sebastian's evasion, and Mathilde displayed small interest in such details. She rather fastened, however, upon the assistance rendered by Louis d'Arragon.

"Why did he do it?" she asked.

"Oh, because I asked him," was the reply.

"And why did you ask him?"

"Who else was there to ask?" returned Désirée, which was indeed unanswerable.

Perhaps the question had been suggested to her by de Casimir, who, on learning that Louis d'Arragon had helped her father to slip through the Emperor's fingers, had asked the same in his own characteristic way.

"What could he hope to gain by doing it?" he had inquired as he walked by Mathilde's side, along the

Pfaffengasse. And he made other interrogations respecting D'Arragon which Mathilde was no more able to satisfy, as he accompanied her to the Frauengasse.

Since that time the dancing-lessons had been resumed to the music of a hired fiddler, and Désirée had once more taken up her household task of making both ends meet. She approached the difficulties as impetuously as ever, and danced the stout pupils round the room with undiminished energy.

"It seems no good at all, your being married," said one of these breathlessly, while Désirée laughingly attended to her dishevelled hair.

"Why not?"

"Because you still make your own dresses and teach dancing," replied the pupil, with a quick sigh at the thought of some smart bursch in the Prussian contingent.

"Ah, but Charles will return a colonel, and I shall bow to you in a silk dress from a chaise and pair —come, left foot first. You are not so tired as you think you are."

For those that are busy, time flies quickly enough. And there is nothing more absorbing than keeping the wolf from the door, else assuredly the hungry thousands would find time to arise and rend the overfed few.

August succeeded a hot July and brought with it Sebastian's curt letter. Sebastian himself—that shadowy father—returned to his home a few hours later. He was not alone, for a heavier step followed his into the passage, and Désirée, always quick to hear and see and act, coming to the head of the stairs, perceived her father looking upwards towards her, while his companion in rough sailor's clothes turned to lay aside the valise he had carried on his shoulder.

Mathilde was close behind Désirée, and Sebastian kissed his daughters with that cold repression of manner which always suggested a strenuous past in which the emotions had been relinquished for ever as an indulgence unfit for a stern and hard-bitten age.

"I took him away and now return him," said the sailor coming forward. Désirée had always known that it was Louis, but Mathilde gave a little start at the sound of the neat clipping French in the mouth of an educated Frenchman so rarely heard in Dantzig—so rarely heard in all broad France to-day.

"Yes—that is true," answered Sebastian, turning to him with a sudden change of manner. There was that in voice and attitude which his hearers had never noted before, although Charles had often evoked something approaching it. It seemed to indicate that, of all the people with whom they had seen their father hold intercourse, Louis d'Arragon was the only man who stood upon equality with him.

"That is true—and at great risk to yourself," he said, not assigning, however, so great an importance

K

to personal danger as men do in these careful days. As he spoke, he took Louis by the arm and by a gesture invited him to precede him upstairs with a suggestion of *camaraderie* somewhat startling in one usually so cold and formal as Antoine Sebastian, the dancing-master of the Frauengasse.

"I was writing to Charles," said Désirée to D'Arragon, when they reached the drawing-room, and, crossing to her own table, she set the papers in order there. These consisted of a number of letters from her husband, read and re-read, it would appear. And the answer to them, a clean sheet of paper bearing only the date and address, lay beneath her hand.

"The courier leaves this evening," she said, with a queer ring of anxiety in her voice, as if she feared that for some reason or another she ran the risk of failing to despatch her letter. She glanced at the clock, and stood, pen in hand, thinking of what she should write.

"May I enclose a line?" asked Louis. "It is not wise, perhaps, for me to address to him a letter —since I am on the other side. It is a small matter of a heritage which he and I divide. I have placed some money in a Dantzig bank for him. He may require it when he returns."

"Then you do not correspond with Charles?" said Mathilde, clearing a space for him on the larger table, and setting before him ink and pens and paper.

"Thank you, Mademoiselle," he said, glancing at her with that light of interest in his dark eyes which she had ignited once before by a question on the only occasion that they had met. He seemed to detect that she was more interested in him than her indifferent manner would appear to indicate. "No, I am a bad correspondent. If Charles and I, in our present circumstances, were to write to each other it could only lead to intrigue, for which I have no taste and Charles no capacity."

"You seem to hint that Charles might have such a taste then," she said, with her quiet smile, as she moved away leaving him to write.

"Charles has probably found out by this time," he answered with the bluntness which he claimed as a prerogative of his calling and nation, "that a soldier of Napoleon's who intrigues will make a better career than one who merely fights."

He took up his pen and wrote with the absorption of one who has but little time and knows exactly what to say. By chance he glanced towards Désirée, who sat at her own table near the window. She was stroking her cheek with the feather of her pen, looking with puzzled eyes at the blank paper before her. Each time D'Arragon dipped his pen he glanced at her, watching her. And Mathilde, with her needle-work, watched them both.

CHAPTER XII.

FROM BORODINO.

However we brave it out, we men are a little breed.

WAR is the gambling of kings. Napoleon, the
arch-gambler, from that Southern sea where men,
lacking cards or dice and the money to buy either,
will yet play a game of chance with the ten fingers
that God gave them for another purpose—Napoleon
had dealt a hand with every monarch in Europe
before he met for the second time that Northern
adversary of cool blood who knew the waiting game.

It is only where the stakes are small that the
leisurely players, idly fingering the fallen cards, return
in fancy to certain points — to this trick trumped
or that chance missed, playing the game over again.
But when the result is great it overshadows the
game, and all men's thoughts fly to speculation on
the future. How will the loser meet his loss?
What use will the winner make of his gain?

The results of the Russian campaign were so
stupendous to history that the historians of the day,

in their bewilderment, sought rather to preserve these than the details of the war. Thus the student of to-day, in piecing together an impression of bygone times, will inevitably find portions of his picture missing. As a matter of fact, no one can say for certain whether Alexander gently led Napoleon onward to Moscow or was himself driven thither in confusion by the conqueror.

A hundred years ago celebrated generals fought a great deal more and talked a great deal less than they do to-day. There were then no bazaars to be opened nor anniversary dinners to be attended. Neither did the shorthand writer find a ready welcome in high places. Thus a successful warrior who had carried out, *tant bien que mal*, an insignificant campaign or an insignificant portion of a campaign, was not compelled to make modest speeches about himself for the rest of his life.

Napoleon's generals were scarcely social lights. Ney, the hero of the retreat, the bravest of the brave, was a rough man who ate horseflesh without troubling to cook it. Rapp, whose dogged defence of an abandoned city is without compare in the story of war, had the manners and the mind of a peasant. These gentlemen dealt more in deeds than in words. They had not much to say for themselves.

As for the Russians, Russia remains at this time

the one European country unhampered and unharassed by a cheap press—the one country where prominent men have a quiet tongue. A hundred years ago Russians did great deeds, and the rest was silence. Neither Kutusoff nor Alexander ever stated clearly whether the retreat to Moscow was intentional or unavoidable; and these are the only men who knew. Perhaps Napoleon knew; at all events, he thought he did, or pretended to think it long afterwards at St. Helena; for Napoleon the Great was a consummate liar.

Be that as it may, the Russians retreated, and the French advanced farther and farther from their base. It was a great army—the greatest ever seen. For Napoleon had eight monarchs serving with the eagles; generals innumerable, many of them immortal— Davoust, the greatest strategist; Prince Eugene, the incomparable lieutenant; Ney, the fearless; four hundred thousand men. And they carried with them only twenty days' provision.

They had marched from the Vistula, full of shipping, across the Pregel, loaded with stores, to the Niemen, where there was no navigation. Dantzig, behind them—that Gibraltar of the North—was stored with provision enough for the whole army. But there was no transport; for the roads of Lithuania were unsuitable for the heavy carts provided.

The country across the Niemen could scarce sustain

its own sparse population, and had nothing to spare for an invading army. This had once been Poland, and was now inimical to Russia; but Russia did not care, and the friendship of Lithuania was like many human friendships which we make sacrifices to preserve—not worth having.

All the while the Russians retreated, and, stranger still, the French followed them, eking out their twenty days' provision.

"I will make them fight a big battle, and beat them," said Napoleon; "and then the Emperor will sue for peace."

But Barclay de Tolly continued to run away from that great battle. Then came the news that Barclay had been deposed; that Kutusoff was coming from the South to take command. It was true enough; and Barclay cheerfully served in a subordinate position to the new chief. September brought great hopes of a battle, for Kutusoff seemed to retreat with less despatch, like a man choosing his ground—Kutusoff, that master of the waiting game.

Early in September Murat, the impetuous leader of the pursuit, complained to Nansouty that a cavalry charge had not been pushed home.

"The horses have no patriotism," replied Nansouty. "The men will fight on empty stomachs, but not the horses."

An ominous reply at the beginning of a campaign, while communications were still open.

At last, within a few days' march of Moscow, Kutusoff made a stand. At last the great battle was imminent, after a hundred false alarms, after many disappointed hopes. The country had been flat hitherto. The Borodino, running in a wider valley than many of these rivers, which are merely great ditches, seemed to offer possibilities of defence. It was the only hope for Moscow.

"At last," wrote Charles to Désirée on September 6, "we are to have a great battle. There has been much fighting the last few days, but I have seen none of it. We are only eighty miles from Moscow. If there is a great battle to-morrow we shall see Moscow in less than a week. For we shall win. I have now found out from one who is near him that the Emperor saw and remembered me the day he passed us in the Frauengasse—our wedding-day, dearest. Nobody is too insignificant for him to know. He thought that my marriage to you (for he knows that you are French) would militate against the work I had been given to do in Dantzig, so he gave orders for me to be sent at once to Königsberg and to continue the work there. De Casimir tells me that the Emperor is pleased with me. De Casimir is the best friend I have; I am sure of that. It is said that under the walls of Moscow the

Emperor will dictate his terms to Alexander. Every one wonders that Alexander of Russia did not make proposals of peace when Vilna and Smolensk fell. In a week we may be at Moscow. In a month I may be back at Dantzig, Désirée. . . ."

And the rest would have been for Désirée's eyes alone, had it ever been penned. For next in sacredness to heaven-inspired words are mere human love-letters; and those who read the love-letters of another commit a sacrilege. But Charles never finished the letter, for the dawn surprised him where he wrote in a shed by the miserable Kalugha, a streamlet running to the Moskwa. And it was the dawn of September 7, 1812.

"There is the sun of Austerlitz," said Napoleon to those who were near him when it arose. But it was not. It was the sun of Borodino. And before it set the great battle desired by the French had been fought, and eight French generals lay dead, while thirty more were wounded. Murat, Davoust, Ney, Junot, Prince Eugene, Napoleon himself—all were there; and all fought to finish a war which from the first had been disliked. The French claimed it as a victory; but they gained nothing by it, and they lost forty thousand killed and wounded.

During the night the Russians evacuated the position which they had held, and lost, and retaken.

They retreated towards Moscow, but Napoleon was hardly ready to pursue.

These things, however, are history, and those who wish to know of them may read them in another volume. While to the many orderly persons who would wish to see everything in its place and the history-books on the top shelf to be taken down and read on a future day (which will never come), to such the explanation is due that this battle of Borodino is here touched upon because it changed the current of some lives with which we have to deal.

For battles and revolutions and historical events of any sort are the jagged instruments with which Fate rough-hews our lives, leaving us to shape them as we will. In other days, no doubt, men rough-hewed, while Fate shaped. But in these gentle times we are so tender, so careful for the individual, that we never cut and slash, but move softly, very tolerant, very easy-going, seeking the compromise that brings peace and breeds a small and timid race of men.

Into such lives Fate comes crashing like a wood-man with his axe, leaving us to smooth the edges of the gaping wound and smile, and say that we are not hurt; to pare away the knots and broken stumps, and hope that our neighbour, concealing such himself, will have the decency to pretend not to see.

Thus the battle of Borodino crashed into the lives

of Désirée and Mathilde, and their father, living quietly on the sunny side of the Frauengasse in Dantzig. Antoine Sebastian was the first to hear the news. He had, it seemed, special facilities for learning news at the Weissen Röss'l, whither he went again now in the evening.

"There has been a great battle," he said, with so much more than his usual self-restraint that Désirée and Mathilde exchanged a glance of anxiety. "A man coming this evening from Dirschau saw and spoke with the Imperial couriers on their way to Berlin and Paris It was a great victory, quite near to Moscow. But the loss on both sides has been terrible."

He paused and glanced at Désirée. It was his creed that good blood should show an example of self-restraint and a certain steadfast, indifferent courage.

"Not so much among the French," he said, "as among the Bavarians and Italians. It is an odd way of showing patriotism, to gain victories for the conqueror. One hoped——" he paused and made a gesture with his right hand, scarcely indicative of a staunch hope, "that the man's star might be setting, but it would appear to be still in the ascendant. Charles," he added, as an afterthought, "would be on the staff. No doubt he only saw the fighting from a distance."

Désirée, from whose face the colour had faded, nodded cheerfully enough.

"Oh yes," she answered, "I have no doubt he is safe. He has good fortune."

For she was an apt pupil, and had already learnt that the world only wishes to leave us in undisputed possession of our anxieties or sorrows, however ready it may be to come forward and take a hand in good fortune.

"But there is no definite news," said Mathilde, hardly looking up from the needlework at which her fingers were so deft and industrious.

"No."

"No news of Charles, I mean," she continued, "or of any of our friends. Of Monsieur de Casimir, for instance?"

"No. As for Colonel de Casimir," returned Sebastian thoughtfully, "he, like Charles, holds some staff appointment of which one does not understand the scope. He is without doubt uninjured."

Mathilde glanced at her father not without suspicion. His grand manner might easily be at times a screen. One never knows how much is perceived by those who look down from a high place.

The town was quiet enough all that night. Sebastian must have heard the news from some unofficial source, for none other seemed to know it. But at daybreak the church bells, so rarely used in Dantzig for rejoicing, awoke the burghers to the fact that the Emperor bade them make merry. Napoleon gave great heed to such matters. In the churches of Lithuania and farther on in Russia he had commanded the popes to pray for him at their altars instead of for the Czar.

When Désirée came downstairs, she found a packet awaiting her. The courier had come in during the night. This was more than a letter. A number of papers had been folded in a handkerchief and bound with string. The address was written on a piece of white leather cut from the uniform of one who had fallen at Borodino, and had no more need of sabretasche or trapping.

" Madame Désirée Darragon—*née* Sebastian,

Frauengasse 36,

Dantzig."

Désirée's heart stood still; for the writing was unknown to her. As she cut the network of string, she thought that Charles was dead. When the enclosed papers fell upon the table, she was sure of it; for they were all in his writing. She did not pick and choose as one would who has leisure and no very strong excitement, but took up the first paper and read:

"Dear C.—I have been fortunate, as you will see from the enclosed report. His Majesty cannot again say that I have been neglectful. I was quite right. It is Sebastian and only Sebastian that we need fear. Here, they are clumsy conspirators compared to him.

I have been in the river half the night, listening at the open stern window of a Reval pink to every word they said. His Majesty can safely come to Konigsberg. Indeed, he is better out of Dantzig. For the whole country is riddled with that which they call patriotism, and we, treason. But I can only repeat what His Majesty disbelieved the day before yesterday —that the heart of the ill is Dantzig, and the venom of it Sebastian. Who he really is and what he is about, you must find out how you can. I go forward to-day to Gumbinnen. The enclosed letter to its address—I beg of you—if only in acknowledgment of all that I have sacrificed."

The letter was unsigned, but the writing was the writing of Charles Darragon, and Désirée knew what he had sacrificed—what he could never recover.

There were two or three more letters addressed to "Dear C.," bearing no signature, and yet written by Charles. Désirée read them carefully with a sort of numb attention which photographed them permanently on her memory like writing that is carved in stone upon a wall. There must be some explanation in one of them. Who had sent them to her? Was Charles dead?

At last she came to a sealed envelope addressed to herself by Charles. Some other hand had copied the address from it in identical terms on the piece of white leather. She opened and read it. It was the letter written to her by Charles on the bank of the Kalugha river on the eve of Borodino, and left unfinished by him. He must be dead. She prayed that he might be.

She was alone in the room, having come down early, as was her wont, to prepare breakfast. She heard Lisa talking with some one at the door—a messenger, no doubt, to say that Charles was dead.

One letter still remained unread. It was in a different writing—the writing on the white leather.

"Madame," it read, "The enclosed papers were found on the field by one of my orderlies. One of them being addressed to you, furnishes a clue to their owner, who must have dropped them in the hurry of the advance. Should Captain Charles Darragon be your husband, I have the pleasure to inform you that he was seen alive and well at the end of the day." The writer assured Désirée of his respectful consideration, and wrote "Surgeon" after his name.

Désirée had read the explanation too late.

CHAPTER XIII.

IN THE DAY OF REJOICING.

Truth, though it crush me

THE door of the room stood open, and the sound of a step in the passage made Désirée glance up, as she hastily put together the papers found on the battlefield of Borodino.

Louis d'Arragon was coming into the room, and for an instant, before his expression changed, she saw all the fatigue that he must have endured during the night; all that he must have risked. His face was usually still and quiet; a combination of that contemplative calm which characterises seafaring faces, and the clean-cut immobility of a racial type developed by hereditary duties of self-restraint and command.

He knew that there had been a battle, and, seeing the papers on the table, his eyes asked her the inevitable question which his lips were slow to put into words.

In reply Désirée shook her head. She looked at the papers in quick thought. Then she withdrew from them the letter written to her by Charles—and put the others together.

"You told me to send for you," she said in a quiet, tired voice, "if I wanted you. You have saved me the trouble."

His eyes were hard with anxiety as he looked at her. She held the letters towards him.

"By coming," she added, with a glance at him which took in the dust, and the stains of salt-water on his clothes, the fatigue he sought to conceal by a rigid stillness, and the tension that was left by the dangers he had passed through—daring all—to come.

Seeing that, he looked doubtfully at the papers, she spoke again.

"One," she said, "that one on the stained paper, is addressed to me. You can read it—since I ask you."

The letter told him, at all events, that Charles was not killed, and, seeing his face clear as he read, she gave an odd, curt laugh.

"Read the others," she said. "Oh! you need not hesitate. You need not be so particular. Read one, the top one. One is enough."

The windows stood open, and the morning breeze fluttering the curtains brought in the gay sound of bells, the high clear bells of Hanseatic days, rejoicing at Napoleon's new success—by order of Napoleon. A bee sailed harmoniously into the room, made the circuit of it, and sought the open again with a hum that faded drowsily into silence.

D'Arragon read the letter slowly from beginning to the unsigned end, while Désirée, sitting at the table, upon which she leant one elbow, resting her small square chin in the palm of her hand, watched him.

"Ah!" she exclaimed at length, with a ring of contempt in her voice, as if at the thought of something unclean. "A spy! It is so easy for you to keep still, and to hide all you feel."

D'Arragon folded the letter slowly. It was the fatal letter written in the upper room in the shoe-maker's house in Königsberg in the Neuer Markt, where the linden trees grow close to the window. In it Charles spoke lightly of the sacrifice he had made in leaving Désirée on his wedding-day, to do the Emperor's bidding. It was indeed the greatest sacrifice that man can make; for he had thrown away his honour.

"It may not be so easy as you think," returned D'Arragon, looking towards the door.

He had no time to say more; for Mathilde and her father were talking together on the stairs as they came down. D'Arragon thrust the letters into his pocket, the only indication he had time to give to Désirée of the policy they must pursue. He stood facing the door, alert and quiet, with only a moment in which to shape the course of more than one life.

"There is good news, Monsieur," he said to Sebastian. "Though I did not come to bring it."

Sebastian pointed interrogatively to the open window, where the sound of the bells seemed to emphasize the sunlight and the freshness of the morning.

"No—not that," returned D'Arragon. "It is a great victory, they tell me; but it is hard to say whether such news would be good or bad. It was of Charles that I spoke. He is safe—Madame has heard."

He spoke rather slowly, and turned towards Désirée with a measured gesture, not unlike Sebastian's habitual manner, and a quick glance to satisfy himself that she had understood and was ready.

"Yes," said Désirée, "he was safe and well after the battle, but he gives no details; for the letter was actually written the day before."

"With a mere word, added in postscriptum, to say that he was unhurt at the end of the day," suggested Sebastian, already drawing forward a chair with a gesture full of hospitality, inviting D'Arragon to be seated at the simple breakfast-table. But D'Arragon was looking at Mathilde, who had gone rather hurriedly to the window, as if to breathe the air. He had caught a glimpse of her face as she passed. It was hard and set, quite colourless, with bright, sleepless eyes. D'Arragon was a sailor. He had seen that look in rougher faces and sterner eyes, and knew what it meant

"No details?" asked Mathilde in a muffled voice, without looking round.

"No," answered Désirée, who had noticed nothing. How much more clearly we should understand what is going on around us if we had no secrets of our own to defend!

In obedience to Sebastian's gesture, D'Arragon took a chair, and even as he did so Mathilde came to the table, calm and mistress of herself again, to pour out the coffee, and do the honours of the simple meal. D'Arragon, besides having acquired the seamen's habit of adapting himself unconsciously and unobtrusively to his surroundings, was of a direct mind, lacking self-consciousness, and simplified by the pressure of a strong and steady purpose. For men's minds are like the atmosphere, which is always cleared by a steady breeze, while a changing wind generates vapours, mist, uncertainty.

"And what news do you bring from the sea?" asked Sebastian. "Is your sky there as overcast as ours in Dantzig?"

"No, Monsieur, our sky is clearing," answered

D'Arragon, eating with a hearty appetite the fresh bread and butter set before him. "Since I saw you, the treaties have been signed, as you doubtless know, between Sweden and Russia and England."

Nodding his head with silent emphasis, Sebastian gave it to be understood that he knew that and more.

"It makes a great difference to us at sea in the Baltic," said D'Arragon. "We are no longer harassed night and day, like a dog, hounded from end to end of a hostile street, not daring to look into any doorway. The Russian ports and Swedish ports are open to us now."

"One is glad to hear that your life is one of less hardship," said Sebastian gravely. "I . . . who have tasted it."

Désirée glanced at his lean, hard face. She rose, went out of the room, and returned in a few minutes carrying a new loaf which she set on the table before him with a short laugh, and something glistening in her eyes that was not mirth.

But neither Désirée nor Mathilde joined in the conversation. They were glad for their father to have a companion so sympathetic as to produce a marked difference in his manner. For Sebastian was more at ease with Louis d'Arragon than he was with Charles, though the latter had the tie of a common fatherland, and spoke the same French that Sebastian spoke.

D'Arragon's French had the roundness always imparted to that language by an English voice. It was perfect enough, but of an educated perfection.

The talk was of such matters as concerned men more than women; of armies and war and treaties of peace. For all the world thought that Alexander of Russia would be brought to his knees by the battle of Borodino. A hundred years ago, moreover, women did not know their place as they do to-day. They ignored the primary ethics of the equality of the sexes, and did not know, as we know to-day, that a woman's opinion is always of immense value, whether she know anything of the matter or not.

Save for the one reference to his life in the Baltic during the past two months, D'Arragon said nothing of himself, of his patient, dogged work carried on by day and by night in all weathers. Content to have escaped with his life, he neither referred to, nor thought of, his part in the negotiations which had resulted in the treaty just signed. For he had been the link between Russia and England; the never-failing messenger passing from one to the other with question and answer which were destined to bear fruit at last in an understanding brought to perfection in Paris, culminating at Elba.

Both were guarded in what they said of passing events, and both seemed to doubt the truth of the reports now flying through the streets of Dantzig. Even in the quiet Frauengasse all the citizens were out on their terraces calling questions to those that passed by beneath the trees. The itinerant tradesman, the milkman going his round, the vendors of fruit from Langfuhr and the distant villages of the plain, lingered at the doors to tell the servants the latest gossip of the market-place. Even in this frontier city, full of spies, strangers spoke together in the streets, and the sound of their voices, raised above the clang of carillons, came in at the open window.

"At first a victory is always a great one," said D'Arragon, looking towards the window.

"It is so easy to ring a bell," added Sebastian, with his rare smile.

He was quite himself this morning, and only once did the dull look arrest his features into the stony stillness which his daughters knew.

"You are the only one of your name in Dantzig," said D'Arragon, in the course of question and answer as to the safe delivery of letters in time of war.

"So far as I know, there is no other Sebastian," replied he; and Désirée, who had guessed the motive of the question, which must have been in D'Arragon's mind from the beginning, was startled by the fulness of the answer. It seemed to make reply to more than D'Arragon had asked. It shattered the last faint hope that there might have been another Sebastian of whom Charles had written.

"For myself," said D'Arragon, changing the subject quickly, "I can now make sure of receiving letters addressed to me in the care of the English Consul at Riga, or the Consul at Stockholm, should you wish to communicate with me, or should Madame find leisure to give me news of her husband."

"Désirée will no doubt take pleasure in keeping you advised of Charles's progress. As for myself, I fear I am a bad correspondent. Perhaps not a desirable one in these days," said Sebastian, his face slowly clearing. He waved the point aside with a gesture that looked out of place on a hand lean and spare, emerging from a shabby brown sleeve without cuff or ruffle.

"For I feel assured," he went on, "that we shall continue to hear good news of your cousin; not only that he is safe and well, but that he makes progress in his profession. He will go far, I am sure."

D'Arragon bowed his acknowledgment of this kind thought, and rose rather hastily.

"My best chance of quitting the city unseen," he said, "is to pass through the gates with the market-people returning to the villages. To do that, I must not delay."

"The streets are so full," replied Sebastian, glancing

out of the window, " that you will pass through them unnoticed. I see beneath the trees, a neighbour, Koch the locksmith, who is perhaps waiting to give me news. While you are saying farewell, I will go out and speak to him. What he has to tell may interest you and your comrades at sea—may help your escape from the city this morning."

He took his hat as he spoke and went to the door. Mathilde, thirsting for the news that seemed to hum in the streets like the sound of bees, rose and followed him. Désirée and D'Arragon were left alone. She had gone to the window, and, turning there, she looked back at him over her shoulder, where he stood by the door watching her.

" So, you see," she said, " there is no other Sebastian."

D'Arragon made no reply. She came nearer to him, her blue eyes sombre with contempt for the man she had married. Suddenly she pointed to the chair which D'Arragon had just vacated.

" That is where he sat. He has eaten my father's salt a hundred times," she said, with a short laugh. For whithersoever civilization may take us, we must still go back to certain primæval laws of justice between man and man.

" You judge too hastily," said D'Arragon; but she interrupted him with a gesture of warning."

"I have not judged hastily," she said. "You do not understand. You think I judge from that letter. That is only a confirmation of something that has been in my mind for a long time—ever since my wedding-day. I knew when you came into the room upstairs on that day that you did not trust Charles."

"I—— ?" he asked.

"Yes," she answered, standing squarely in front of him and looking him in the eyes. "You did not trust him. You were not glad that I had married him. I could see it in your face. I have never forgotten."

D'Arragon turned away towards the window. Sebastian and Mathilde were in the street below, in the shade of the trees, talking with the eager neighbours.

"You would have stopped it if you could," said Désirée; and he did not deny it.

"It was some instinct," he said at length. "Some passing misgiving."

"For Charles?" she asked sharply.

And D'Arragon, looking out of the window, would not answer. She gave a sudden laugh.

"One cannot compliment you on your politeness," she said. "Was it for Charles that you had misgivings?"

At last D'Arragon turned on his heel.

"Does it matter?" he asked. "Since I came too late."

"That is true," she said, after a pause. "You came too late; so it doesn't matter. And the thing is done now, and I . . . , well, I suppose I must do what others have done before me—I must make the best of it."

"I will help you," said D'Arragon slowly, almost carefully, "if I can."

He was still avoiding her eyes, still looking out of the window. Sebastian was coming up the steps.

CHAPTER XIV.

MOSCOW.

Nothing is so disappointing as failure—except success.

WHILE the Dantzigers with grave faces discussed the news of Borodino beneath the trees in the Frauengasse, Charles Darragon, white with dust, rose in his stirrups to catch the first sight of the domes and cupolas of Moscow.

It was a sunny morning, and the gold on the churches gleamed and glittered in the shimmering heat like fairyland. Charles had ridden to the summit of a hill and sat for a moment, as others had done, in silent contemplation. Moscow at last! All around him men were shouting: "Moscow! Moscow!" Grave, white-haired generals waved their shakos in the air. Those at the summit of the hill called the others to come. Far down in the valley, where the dust raised by thousands of feet hung in the air like a mist, a faint sound like the roar of falling water could be heard. It was the word "Moscow!" sweeping back to the rearmost ranks of these starving men who had marched for two months beneath the glaring sun, parched with dust, through a country that seemed to them a Sahara. Every house they approached, they had found deserted. Every barn was empty. The very crops ripening to harvest had been gathered in and burnt. Near to the miserable farmhouses, a pile of ashes hardly cold marked where the poor furniture had been tossed upon the fire kindled with the year's harvest.

Everywhere it was the same. There are, as God created it, few countries of a sadder aspect than that which spreads between the Moskwa and the Vistula. But it has been decreed by the dim laws of Race that the ugly countries shall be blessed with the greater love of their children, while men born in a beautiful land seem readiest to emigrate from it and make the best settlers in a new home. There is only one country in the world with a ring-fence round it. If a Russian is driven from his home, he will go to another part of Russia : there is always room.

Before the advance of the spoilers, chartered by their leader to unlimited and open rapine—indeed, he had led them hither with that understanding—the Russians, peasant and noble alike, fled to the East. A hundred times the advance guard, fully alive to the advantages of their position, had raced to the gates of a château only to find, on breaking open the doors, that it was empty—the furniture destroyed, the stores burnt, the wine poured out.

So also in the peasants' huts. Some, more careful than the rest, had pulled the thatch from the roof to burn it. There was no corn in this the Egypt of their greedy hopes. And, lest they should bring the corn with them, the spoilers found the mills everywhere wrecked.

It was something new to them. It was new to Napoleon, who had so frequently been met halfway, who knew that men for greed will part smilingly with half in order to save the residue. He knew that many, rather than help a neighbour who is in danger by a robber, will join the robber and share the spoil, crying out that *force majeure* was used to them.

But, as every man must judge according to his lights, so must even the greatest find himself in the dark at last. No man of the Latin race will ever understand the Slav. And because the beginning is easy—because in certain superficial tricks of speech and thought Paris and Petersburg are not unlike—so much the more is the breach widened when necessity digs deeper than the surface. For, to make the acquaintance of a stranger who seems to be a counterpart of one's self in thought and taste, is like the first hearing of a kindred language such as Dutch to the English ear. At first it sounds like one's own tongue

MOSCOW. 159

with a hundred identical words, but on closer listening it will be found that the words mean something else, and that the whole is incomprehensible and the more difficult to acquire by the very reason of its resemblance.

Napoleon thought that the Russians would act as his enemies of the Latin race had acted. He thought that like his own people they would be over-confident, urging each other on to great deeds by loud words and a hundred boasts. But the Russians lack self-confidence, are timid rather than over-bold, dreamy rather than fiery. Only their women are glib of speech. He thought that they would begin very brilliantly and end with a compromise, heart-breaking at first and soon lived down.

"They are savages out here in the plains," he said. "It is a barbaric and stupid instinct that makes them destroy their own property for the sake of hampering us. As we approach Moscow we shall find that the more civilized inhabitants of the villages, enervated by an easy life, rendered selfish by possession of wealth, will not abandon their property, but will barter and sell to us and find themselves the victims of our might."

And the army believed him. For they always believed him. Faith can, indeed, move mountains. It carried four hundred thousand men, without provisions, through a barren land.

And now, in sight of the golden city, the army was still hungry. Nay! it was ragged already. In three columns it converged on the doomed capital, driving before it like a swarm of flies the Cossacks who harassed the advance.

Here again, on the hill looking down into the smiling valley of the Moskwa, the unexpected awaited the invaders. The city, shimmering in the sunlight like the realization of some Arab's dream, was silent. The Cossacks had disappeared. Except those around the Kremlin, towering above the river, the city had no walls.

The army halted while aides-de-camp flew hither and thither on their weary horses. Charles Darragon, sunburnt, dusty, hoarse with cheering, was among the first. He looked right and left for de Casimir, but could not see him. He had not seen his chief since Borodino, for he was temporarily attached to the staff of Prince Eugene, who had lost heavily at the Kalugha river.

It was usual for the army to halt before a beleaguered city and await the advent in all humility of the vanquished. Commonly it was the mayor of a town who came, followed by his councillors in their robes, to explain that the army had abandoned the city, which now begged to throw itself upon the mercy of the conqueror.

For this the army waited on that sunny September morning.

"He is putting on his robes," they said gaily. "He is new to this work."

But the mayor of Moscow disappointed them. At last the troops moved on and camped for the night in a village under the Kremlin walls. It was here that Charles received a note from de Casimir.

"I am slightly wounded," wrote that officer, "but am following the army. At Borodino my horse was killed under me, and I was thrown. While I was insensible, I was robbed and lost what money I had, as well as my despatch-case. In the latter was the letter you wrote to your wife. It is lost, my friend; you must write another."

Charles was tired. He would put off till to-morrow, he thought, and write to Désirée from Moscow. As he lay, all dressed on the hard ground, he fell to thinking of what he should write to Désirée to-morrow from Moscow. The mere date and address of such a letter would make her love him the more, he thought; for, like his leaders, he was dazed by a surfeit of glory.

As he fell asleep smiling at these happy reflections, Désirée, far away in Dantzig, was locking in her bureau the letter which had been lost and found again; while, on the deck of his ship, lifting gently to the tideway where the Vistula sweeps out into the Dantziger Bucht, Louis d'Arragon stood fingering reflectively in his jacket-pocket the unread papers which had fallen from the same despatch-case. For it is a very small world in which to do wrong, though if a man do a little good in his lifetime it is—heaven knows—soon mislaid and trodden under the feet of the new-comers.

The next day it was definitely ascertained that the citizens of Moscow had no communication to make to the conquering leaders. Soon after daylight the army moved towards the city. The suburbs were deserted. The houses stood with closed shutters and locked doors. Not so much as a dog awaited the triumphant entry through the city gates.

Long streets without a living being from end to end met the eyes of those daring organizers of triumphal entries who had been sent forward to clear a path and range the respectful citizens on either hand. But there were no citizens. There was not a single witness to this triumph of the greatest army the world had seen, led across Europe by the first captain in all history to conquer a virgin capital.

The various corps marched to their quarters in silence, with nervous glances at the shuttered windows. Some, breaking rank, ventured into the churches which stood open. The candles were lighted on the altars, they reported to their comrades in a hushed voice when they returned, but there was no one there.

Certain palaces were selected as head-quarters for the general officers and the chiefs of various departments. As often as not a summons would be answered and the door opened by an obsequious porter, who handed the keys to the first-comer. But he spoke no French, and only cringed in silence when addressed. Other doors were broken in.

It was like a play acted in dumb show on an immense stage. It was disquieting and incomprehensible even to the oldest campaigner, while the young fire-eaters, fresh from St. Cyr, were strangely depressed by it. There was a smell of sour smoke in the air, a suggestion of inevitable tragedy.

On the Krasnaya Plòschad—the great Red Square, which is the central point of the old town—the soldiers were already buying and selling the spoil wrested from the burning Exchange. It seemed that the citizens before leaving had collected their merchandise in this building to burn it. To the rank-and-file this meant nothing but an incomprehensible stupidity. To the educated and the thoughtful it was another evidence of that dumb and sullen capacity for infinite self-sacrifice which makes Russians different from any other race, and which has yet to be reckoned with in the history of the world. For it will tend to the greatest good of the greatest number, and is a power for national aggrandisement quite unattainable by any Latin people.

Charles, with the other officers of Prince Eugene's staff, was quartered in a palace on the Petrovka—that wide street running from the Kremlin northward to the boulevards and the parks. Going towards it he passed through the bazaars and the merchants' quarters, where, like an army of rag-pickers, the eager looters were silently hurrying from heap to heap. Every warehouse had, it seemed, been ransacked and its contents thrown out into the streets. The first-comers had hurried on, seeking something more valuable, more portable, leaving the later arrivals to turn over their garbage like dogs upon a dust-heap.

The Petrovka is a long street of great houses, and was now deserted. The pillagers were nervous and ill at ease, as men must always be in the presence of something they do not understand. The most experienced of them—and there were some famous robbers in Murat's vanguard—had never seen an empty city abandoned all standing, as the Russians had abandoned Moscow. They felt apprehensive of the unknown. Even the least imaginative of them looked askance at the tall houses, at the open doors of the empty churches, and they kept together for company's sake.

Charles's rooms were in the Momonoff Palace, where even the youngest lieutenant had vast apartments assigned to him. It was in one of these— a lady's boudoir, where his dust-covered baggage had been thrown down carelessly by his orderly on a blue satin sofa—that he sat down to write to Désirée.

His emotions had been stirred by all that he had passed through—by the first sight of Moscow, by the passage beneath the Gate of the Redeemer, where every man must uncover and only Napoleon dared to wear a hat; by the bewildering sense of triumph and the knowledge that he was taking part in one of the epochs of man's history on this earth. The emotions lie very near together, so that laughter being aroused must also touch on tears, and hatred being kindled warms the heart to love.

And, here in this unknown woman's room, with the very pen that she had thrown aside, Charles, who wrote and spoke his love with such facility, wrote to Désirée a love-letter such as he had never written before.

When it was sealed and addressed he called his orderly to take it to the officer to whose duty it fell to make up the courier for Germany. But he received no reply. The man had joined his comrades in the busier quarters of the city. Charles went to the head of the stairs and called again, with no better success.

The house was comparatively modern, built on the familiar lines of a Parisian *hôtel*, with a wide stair descending to an entrance archway where carriages passed through into a courtyard.

Descending the stairs, Charles found that even the sentry had absented himself from his duty. His chassepot, leant against the post of the stone doorway, indicated that he was not far. Listening in the silence of that great house, Charles heard some one at work with hammer and chisel in the courtyard. He went there, and found the sentry kneeling at a low door, endeavouring to break it open. The man had not been idle; from a piece of rope slung across his back half a dozen clocks were suspended. They rattled together like the wares of a travelling tinsmith at every movement of his arms.

"What are you doing there, my friend?" asked Charles.

The man held up one finger over his shoulder without looking round, and shook it from side to side, as not desiring to be interrupted.

"The cellar," he answered, "always the cellar. It is human nature. We get it from the animals."

He glanced round as he worked, and, perceiving that he had been addressing an officer, he scrambled to his feet with a grumbled curse. He was an old man, baked by the sun. The wrinkles in his face were filled with dust. Since quitting the banks of the Vistula no opportunity for ablution seemed to have presented itself to him. He stood at attention, his lips working over sunken gums.

"I want you to take this letter," said Charles, "to the officer on service at head-quarters, and ask him to include it in his courier. It is, as you see, a private letter—to my wife at Dantzig."

The man looked at it, and grumbled something inaudible. He took it in his hand and turned it over with the slow manner of the illiterate.

CHAPTER XV.

THE GOAL.

God writes straight on crooked lines.

CHARLES, having given his letter to the sentry with the order to take it to its immediate destination, turned towards the stairs again. In those days an order was given in a different tone to that which servitude demands in later times.

He returned to his room on the first floor without even waiting to make sure that he would be obeyed. He had scarcely seated himself when, after a fumbling knock, the sentry opened the door and followed him into the room, still holding the letter in his hand.

"Mon capitaine," he said with a certain calmness of manner as from an old soldier to a young one, "a word—that is all. This letter," he turned it in his hand as he spoke, and looking at Charles beneath scowling brows, awaited an explanation. "Did you pick it up?"

"No—I wrote it."

"Good. I . . ." he paused, and tapped himself

on the chest so that there could be no mistake; there was a rattling sound behind him suggestive of iron-ware. Indeed, he was hung about with other things than clocks, and seemed to be of opinion that if a soldier sets value upon any object he must attach it to his person. "I, Barlasch of the Guard—Marengo, the Danube, Egypt—picked up after Borodino a letter like it. I cannot read very quickly—indeed—— Bah! the old Guard needs no pens and paper—but that letter I picked up was just like this"

"Was it addressed like that to Madame Désirée Darragon?"

"So a comrade told me. It is you, her husband?"

"Yes," answered Charles, "since you ask; I am her husband."

"Ah!" replied Barlasch darkly, and his limbs and features settled themselves into a patient waiting.

"Well," asked Charles, "what are you waiting for?"

"Whatever you may think proper, mon capitaine, for I gave the letter to the surgeon who promised that it should be forwarded to its address."

Charles laughingly sought his purse. But there was nothing in it, so he looked round the room.

"Here, add this to your collection," and he took a small French clock from the writing-table, a pretty, gilded toy from Paris.

"Thank you, mon capitaine."

Barlasch, with shaking fingers, unknotted the rope around his shoulders. As he was doing so one of the clocks on his back began to strike. He paused, and stood looking gravely at his superior officer. Another clock took up the tale and a third, while Barlasch sternly stood at attention.

"Four o'clock," he said to himself, "and I, who have not yet breakfasted——"

With a grunt and a salute he turned towards the door which stood open. Some one was coming up the stairs rather slowly, his spurs clinking, his scabbard clashing against the gilded banisters. Papa Barlasch stood aside at attention, and Colonel de Casimir came into the room with a gay word of greeting. Barlasch went out, but he did not close the door. It is to be presumed that he stood without, where he might have overheard all that they said to each other for quite a long time, until it was almost the half-hour when the clocks would strike again. But de Casimir, perceiving that the door was open, closed it quietly from within, and Barlasch, shut out on the wide landing, made a grimace at the massive woodwork before turning to descend the stairs.

It was the middle of September, and the days were shortening. The dusk of evening had already closed over the city when de Casimir and Charles at length came downstairs. No one had troubled to open the shutters of such rooms as were not required ; and these were many. For Moscow was even at that day a great city, though less spacious and more fantastic than it is to-day. There was plenty of room for the whole army in the houses left empty by their owners, so that many lodged as they had never lodged before and would never lodge again.

The stairs were almost dark when Charles and his companion descended them. The rusted musket poised against the doorpost still indicated the supposed presence of a sentry.

"Listen," said Charles, "I found him burrowing like a rat at a cellar-door in the courtyard. Perhaps he has got in."

They listened, but could hear nothing. Charles led the way towards the courtyard. A glimmer of light guided him to the door he sought. It stood open. Barlasch had succeeded in effecting an entry to the cellar, where his experience taught him to seek the best that an abandoned house contains.

Charles and de Casimir peered down the narrow stairs. By the light of a candle Barlasch was working vigorously amid a confused pile of cases, and furniture, and roughly tied bundles of clothing. He had laid aside nothing, and his movements were attended by the usual rattle of hollow-ware. They could see the perspiration gleaming on his face. Even in this cellar there lingered the faint smell of sour smoke that filled the air of Moscow.

De Casimir caught the gleam of jewellery, and went hurriedly downstairs.

"What are you doing there, my friend?" he asked, and the words were scarcely out of his mouth, when Barlasch extinguished his candle. There followed a dead silence, such as comes when a rodent is disturbed at his work. The two men on the cellar-stairs were conscious of the gaze of the bright, rat-like eyes below.

De Casimir turned and followed Charles upstairs again.

"Come up," he said, "and go to your post."

There was no movement in response.

"Name of a dog," cried de Casimir, "is all discipline relaxed? Come up, I tell you, and obey my orders."

He emphasized his command with the cocking of a pistol, and a slight disturbance in the darkness of the cellar heralded the unwilling approach of Barlasch, who climbed the stairs step by step like a schoolboy coming to punishment.

"It is I who found the door, mon colonel, behind that pile of firewood. It is I who opened it. What is down there is mine," he said, sullenly. But the only reply that de Casimir made was to seize him by the arm and jerk him away from the stairs.

"To your post," he said, "take your arm, and out

into the street, in front of the house. That is your place."

But while he was still speaking, they were all startled by a sudden disturbance in the cellar, and in the gloom a man stumbled up the stairs and ran past them. Barlasch had taken the precaution of bolting the huge front door, which was large enough to give passage to a carriage. The man, who exhaled an atmosphere of dust mingled with the disquieting and all-pervading odour of smoke, rushed at the huge door and tugged furiously at its handles.

Charles, who was on his heels, grasped his arm, but the man swung round and threw him off as if he were a child. He had a hatchet in his hand with which he aimed a blow at Charles, but missed him. Barlasch was already going towards his musket, which stood in the corner against the door-post, but the Russian saw his movement, and forestalled him. Seizing the gun, he presented the bayonet to them, and stood with his back to the door, facing the three men in a breathless silence. He was a large man, dishevelled, with long hair tumbled about his head, and light-coloured eyes, glaring like the eyes of a beast at bay.

In the background de Casimir, quick and calm, had already covered him with the pistol produced as a persuasive to Barlasch. For a second there was silence, during which they all could hear the call to arms in the street outside. The patrol was hurrying down the Petrovka, calling the assembly.

The report of the pistol rang through the house, shaking the doors and windows. The man threw up his arms and stood for a moment looking at de Casimir with an expression of blank amazement. Then his legs seemed to slip away from beneath him, and he collapsed to the floor. He turned over with movements singularly suggestive of a child seeking a comfortable position in bed, and lay quite still, his cheek on the pavement and his staring eyes turned towards the cellar-door from which he had emerged.

"He has his affair—that parishioner," muttered Barlasch, looking at him with a smile that twisted his mouth to one side. And, as he spoke, the man's throat rattled. De Casimir was reloading his pistol. So persistent was the gaze of the dead man's eyes that de Casimir turned on his heel to look in the same direction.

"Quick!" he exclaimed, pointing to the doorway, from which a lazy white smoke emerged in thin puffs. "Quick, he has set fire to the house!"

"Quick—with what, mon colonel?" asked Barlasch.

"Why, go and fetch some men with a fire-engine."

"There are no fire-engines left in Moscow, mon colonel!"

"Then find buckets, and tell me where the well is."

"There are no buckets left in Moscow, mon colonel. We found that out last night, when we wanted to water the horses. The citizens have removed them. And there is not a well of which the rope has not been cut. They are droll companions, these Russians, I can tell you."

"Do as I tell you," repeated de Casimir, angrily, "or I shall put you under arrest. Go and fetch men to help me to extinguish this fire."

By way of reply, Barlasch held up one finger in a childlike gesture of attention to some distant sound.

"No, thank you," he said, coolly, "not for me. Discipline, mon colonel, discipline. Listen, you can hear the 'assembly' as well as I. It is the Emperor that one obeys. One thinks of one's military career."

With knotted and shaking fingers he drew back the bolts and opened the door. On the threshold he saluted.

"It is the call to arms, mes officiers," he said. Then, shouldering his rifle, he turned away, and all his clocks struck six. The bells of the city churches seemed to greet him as he stepped into the street, for in Moscow each hour is proclaimed with deafening iteration from a thousand towers.

He looked down the Petrovka; from half the houses which bordered the wide roadway—a street of palaces—the smoke was pouring forth in puffs. He went uphill towards the Red Square and the Kremlin, where the Emperor had his head-quarters. It was to this centre that the patrols had converged. Looking back, Barlasch saw, not one house on fire, but a hundred. The smoke arose from every quarter of the city at once. He hurried on, but was stopped by a crowd of soldiers, all laden with booty, gesticulating, shouting, abusing one another. It was Babel over again. The riff-raff of sixteen nations had followed Napoleon to Moscow—to rob. Half a dozen different tongues were spoken in one army corps. There remained no national pride to act as a deterrent. No man cared what he did. The blame would be laid upon France.

The crowd was collected in front of a high, many-windowed building in flames.

"What is it?" Barlasch asked first one and then another. But no one spoke his tongue. At last he found a Frenchman.

"It is the hospital."

"And what is that smell? What is burning there?"

"Twelve thousand wounded," answered the man, with a sickening laugh. And even as he spoke one or two of the wounded dragged themselves, half burnt, down the wide steps. No one dared to approach them, for the walls of the building were already bulging outwards. One man was half covered with a sheet which was black, and his bare limbs were black with smoke. All the hair was burnt from his head and face. He stood for a moment in the doorway— a sight never to be forgotten—and then fell headlong down the steps, where he lay motionless. Some one in the crowd laughed—a high cackle which was heard above the roar of the fire and the deafening chorus of burning timbers.

Barlasch passed on, following some officers who were leading their horses towards the Kremlin. The streets were full of soldiers carrying burdens, and staggering beneath the weight of their spoil. Many were wearing priceless fur cloaks, and others walked in women's wraps of sable and ermine. Some wore jewellery, such as necklaces, on their rough uniforms, and bracelets round their sunburnt wrists. No one laughed at them, but only glanced enviously at the pillage. All were in deadly earnest, and none graver than those who had found drink and now regretted that they had given way to the temptation; for their sober comrades had outwitted them in finding treasure.

One man gravely wore a gilt coronet crammed over the crown of his shako. He joined Barlasch, staggering along beside him.

"I come from the Cathedral," he explained,

confidentially. "St. Michael they call it. They said there was great treasure there hidden in the cellars, but I only found a company of old kings in their coffins. We stirred them up. They were quiet enough when we found them, under their counterpanes of red velvet. We stirred them up with the bayonet, and the dust got into our throats and choked us. Name of God, I am thirsty. You have nothing in your bottle, comrade? No."

Barlasch trudged on, all his possessions swinging and clanking together. The confidential man turned towards him and lifted his water-bottle, weighed it, and found it wanting.

"Name of a name, of a name, of a name," he muttered, walking on. "Yes, there was nothing there. Even the silver plates on the coffins with the names of those gentlemen were no thicker than a sword. But I found a crown in the church itself. I borrowed it from St Michael. He had a sword in his hand, but he did not strike. No. And there was only tinsel on the hilt. No jewels."

He walked on in silence for a few minutes, coughing out the smoke and dust from his lungs. It was almost dark, but the whole city was blazing now, and the sky glowed with a red light that mingled with the remnants of a lurid sunset. A strong wind blew the smoke and the flying sparks across the roofs.

"Then I went into the sacristy," continued the man, stumbling over the dead body of a young girl and turning to curse her. Barlasch looked at him sideways and cursed him for doing it, with a sudden fierce eloquence. For Papa Barlasch was a man of unclean lips.

"There was an old man in there, a sacristan. I asked him where he kept the dishes, and he said he could not speak French. I jerked my bayonet into him—name of a name! he soon spoke French."

Barlasch broke off these delicate confidences by a quick word of command, and himself stood rigid in the roadway before the Imperial Palace of the Kremlin, presenting arms. A man passed close by them on his way towards a waiting carriage. He was stout and heavy-shouldered, peculiarly square, with a thick neck and head set low in the shoulders. On the step of the carriage he turned and surveyed the lurid sky and the burning city to the east with an indifferent air. Into his deep bloodshot eyes there flashed a sudden gleam of life and power, as he glanced along the row of watching faces to read what was written there.

It was Napoleon, at the summit of his dream, hurriedly quitting the Kremlin, the boasted goal of his ambition, after having passed but one night under that proud roof.

CHAPTER XVI.

THE FIRST OF THE EBB.

Tho' he trip and fall
He shall not blind his soul with clay.

THE days were short, and November was drawing to its end when Barlasch returned to Dantzig. Already the frost, holding its own against a sun that seemed to linger in the North that year, exercised its sway almost to midday, and drew a mist from the level plains.

The autumn had been one of unprecedented splendour, making the imaginative whisper that Napoleon, like a second Joshua, could exact obedience even from the sun. A month earlier, soon after the retreat was ordered, the nights had begun to be cold, but the days remained brilliant. Now the rivers were shrouded in white mist, and still water was frozen.

Barlasch seemed to take it for understood that a billet holds good throughout a whole campaign. But the door of No. 36 Frauengasse was locked when he turned its iron handle. He knocked, and waited on the step.

It was Désirée who opened the door at length—
Désirée, grown older, with something new in her eyes.
Barlasch, sure of his *entrée*, had already removed his
boots, which he carried in his hand; this added to a
certain surreptitiousness in his attitude. A handkerchief was bound over his left eye. He wore his shako
still, but the rest of his uniform verged on the fantastic. Under a light-blue Bavarian cavalry cape he
wore a peasant's homespun shirt, and he carried no arms.

He pushed past Désirée rather unceremoniously,
glad to get within doors. He was very lame, and of
his blue knitted stockings only the legs remained; he
was barefoot.

He limped towards the kitchen, glancing over his
shoulder to make sure that Désirée shut the door. The
chair he had made his own stood just within the open
door of the kitchen. It was nine o'clock in the morning, and Lisa had gone to market. Barlasch sat down.

"Voilà," he said, and that was all. But by a
gesture he described the end of the world. Then he
scowled at her with his available eye with suspicion,
and she turned away suddenly, as one may who has
not a clear conscience.

"What is the matter with your eye?" she asked,
in order to break the silence. He laid aside his hat,
and his ragged hair, quite white, fell to his shoulders.
By way of answer, he unknotted the bloodstained dusky

handkerchief, and looked up at her. The hidden eye was uninjured and as bright as the other.

"Nothing," he answered, and he confirmed the statement by a low-born wink. More than once he glanced, with a glaring light in his eye, towards the cupboard where Lisa kept the bread, and quite suddenly Désirée knew that he was starving. She ran to the cupboard, and hurriedly set down on the table before him what was there. It was not much—a piece of cold meat and a whole loaf.

He had taken off his haversack, and was fumbling in it with unsteady hands. At last he found that which he sought. It was wrapped in a silk scarf that must have come from Cashmere to Moscow, and from Moscow in his haversack with pieces of horseflesh and muddy roots to Dantzig. With that awkwardness in giving and taking which belongs to his class, he held out to Désirée a little square "ikon" no bigger than a playing-card. It was of gold, set with diamonds, and the faces of the Virgin and Child were painted with exquisite delicacy.

"It is a thing to say your prayers to," he said gruffly.

By an effort he kept his eyes averted from the food on the table.

"I met a baker on the bridge," he said, "and offered it to him for a loaf, but he refused."

And there was a whole history of human suffering and temptation—of the human fall—in his curt laugh. While Désirée was looking at the treasure in speechless admiration, he turned suddenly and took the bread and meat in his grimy hands. His crooked fingers closed over the loaf, making the crust crack, and for a second the expression of his face was not human. Then he hurried to the room that had been his, like a dog that seeks to hide its greed in its kennel.

In a surprisingly short time he came back, the greyness all gone from his face, though his eyes still glittered with the dry, hard light of starvation. He went back to the chair near the door, and sat down.

"Seven hundred miles," he said, looking down at his feet with a shake of the head, "seven hundred miles in six weeks."

Then he glanced at her and out through the open door, to make sure none could overhear.

"Because I was afraid," he added in a whisper. "I am easily frightened. I am not brave."

Désirée shook her head and laughed. Women have from all time accepted the theory that a uniform makes a man courageous.

"They had to abandon the guns," he went on, "soon after quitting Moscow. The horses were starving. There was a steep hill, and the guns were left at the bottom. Then I began to be afraid. There were some marching with candelabras on their backs and nothing in their *carnassières*. They carried a million francs on their shoulders and death in their faces. I was afraid. I carried salt—salt—and nothing else. Then one day I saw the Emperor's face. That was enough. The same night I crept away while the others slept round the fire. They looked like a masquerade. Some of them wore ermine. Oh! I was afraid, I tell you. I only had the salt and some horse. There was plenty of that on the road. And that toy. I found it in Moscow. I stood in a cellar, as big as this room, full of such things. But one thinks of one's life. I only carried salt, and that picture for you . . . to say your prayers to. The good God will hear you, perhaps; He has no time to listen to us others."

And he used the last words as a French peasant, which is a survival of serfdom that has come down through the furnace of the Revolution.

"But I cannot take it," said Désirée. "It is worth a million francs."

He looked at her fiercely.

"You think that I look for something in return?"

"Oh no!" she answered. "I have nothing to give you in return. I am as poor as you."

"Then we can be friends," he said. He was eyeing

surreptitiously a mug of beer which Désirée had set before him on the table. Some instinct, or the teaching of the last two months, made it repugnant to him to eat or drink beneath his neighbour's eye. He was a sorry-looking figure, not far removed from the animals, and in his downward journey he had picked up, perhaps, the instinct which none can explain, telling an animal to take its food in secret.

Désirée went to the window, turning her back to him, and looked out into the yard. She heard him drink, and set the mug down again with a gulp.

"You were in Moscow?" she said at length, half turning towards him so that he could see her profile and her short upper lip, which was parted as if to ask a question which she did not put into words. He looked her slowly up and down beneath his heavy eyebrows, his little cunning eyes alight with suspicion. He watched her parted lips, which were tilted at the corners, showing humour and a nature quick to laugh or suffer. Then he jerked his head upwards as if he saw the unasked question quivering there, and bore her some malice for her silence.

"Yes! I was in Moscow," he said, watching the colour fade from her face. "And I saw him—your husband—there. I was on guard outside his door the night we entered the city. It was I who carried to the post the letter he wrote you. He was very anxious that it should reach you. You received it— that love-letter?"

"Yes," answered Désirée gravely, in no wise responding to a sudden forced gaiety in Papa Barlasch, which was only an evidence of the shyness with which rough men all the world over approach the subject of love, lacking the refinement with which half-educated women in these days strip it bare and pick it to pieces on the housetops, so that there shall be no glamour left in it.

"I never saw him again," went on Barlasch, "for the 'general' sounded, and I went out into the streets to find the city on fire. In a great army, as in a large country, one may easily lose one's own brother. But he will return—have no fear. He has good fortune —the fine gentleman."

He stopped and scratched his head, looked at her sideways with a grimace of bewilderment.

"It is good news I bring you," he muttered. "He was alive and well when we began the retreat. He was on the staff, and the staff had horses and carriages. They had bread to eat, I am told."

"And you—what had you?" asked Désirée, over her shoulder.

"No matter," he answered gruffly, "since I am here."

"And yet you believe in that man still," flashed out Désirée, turning to face him.

Barlasch held up a warning finger, as if bidding her to be silent on a subject on which she was not capable of forming a judgment. He wagged his head from side to side and heaved a sigh.

"I tell you," he said, "I saw his face after Malo-Jaroslavetz; we lost ten thousand that day. And I was afraid. For I saw in it that he was going to leave us as he did in Egypt. I am not afraid when he is there—not afraid of the Devil—or the bon Dieu, but when Napoleon is not there——" He broke off with a gesture describing abject terror.

"They say in Dantzig," said Désirée, "that he will never get back across the Bérésina, for the Russians are bringing two armies to stop him there. They say that the Prussians will turn against him."

"Ah—they say that already?"

"Yes."

He looked at her with a sudden light of anger in his eyes.

"Who has taught you to hate Napoleon?" he asked bluntly.

And again Désirée turned away from his glance as if she could not meet it.

"No one," she answered.

"It is not the patron," said Barlasch, muttering his thoughts as he hobbled to the door of his little room, and began unloading his belongings with a view to ablution; for he was a self-contained traveller, carrying with him all he required. "It is not the patron. Because such a hatred as his cannot be spoken of. It is not your husband, because Napoleon is his god."

He broke off with one of his violent jerks of the head, almost threatening to dislocate his neck, and looked at her fixedly.

"It is because you have grown into a woman since I went away."

And out came his accusing finger, though Désirée had her back turned towards him, and there was none other to see.

"Ah!" he said, with deadly contempt, "I see. I see!"

"Did you expect me to grow up into a man?" asked Désirée, over her shoulder.

Barlasch stood in the doorway, his lips and jaw moving as if he were masticating wingèd words. At length, having failed to find a tremendous answer, he softly closed the door.

This was not the only wise old veteran of the Grand Army to see which way the wind blew; for many another after the battle of Malo-Jaroslavetz packed upon his back such spoil as he could carry, and set off on foot for France. For the cold had come at length, and not a horse in the French army

was roughed for the snowy roads, nor, indeed, had
provision been made to rough them. This was a sign
not lost upon those who had horses to care for. The
Emperor, who forgot nothing, had forgotten this. He
who foresaw everything, had omitted to foresee the
winter. He had ordered a retreat from Moscow, in
the middle of October, of an army in summer clothing,
without provision for the road. The only hope was
to retreat through a new line of country not despoiled
by the enormous army in its advance of every grain
of corn, every blade of grass. But this hope was
frustrated by the Russians who, hemming them in,
forced them to keep the road along which they had
made so triumphant a march on Moscow.

Already, in the ranks, it was whispered that by
the light of the burning city some had perceived dark
forms moving on the distant plains—a Russian army
passing westward in front of them to await and cut
them off at the passage of some river. The Russians
had fought well at Borodino: they fought desperately
at Malo-Jaroslavetz, which town was taken and retaken
eleven times and left in cinders.

The Grand Army was no longer in a position to
choose its way. It was forced to cross again the
battlefield of Borodino, where thirty thousand dead
lay yet unburied. But Napoleon was still with them,
his genius flashing out at times with something of

the fire which had taken men's breath away and burnt his name indelibly into the pages of the world's history. Even when hard pressed, he never missed a chance of attacking. The enemy never made a mistake that he did not give them reason to rue it.

To the waiting world came at length the news that the winter, so long retarded, had closed down over Russia. In Dantzig, so near the frontier, a hundred rumours chased each other through the streets; and day by day Antoine Sebastian grew younger and gayer. It seemed as if a weight long laid upon his heart had been lifted at last. He made a journey to Königsberg soon after Barlasch's return, and came back with eager eyes. His correspondence was enormous. He had, it seemed, a hundred friends who gave him news and asked something in exchange— advice, encouragement, warning. And all the while men whispered that Prussia would ally herself to Russia, Sweden, and England.

From Paris came news of a growing discontent. For France, among a multitude of virtues, has one vice unpardonable to Northern men: she turns from a fallen friend.

Soon followed the news of Bérésina—a poor little river of Lithuania—where the history of the world hung for a day as on a thread. But a flash of the dying genius surmounted superhuman difficulties, and the catastrophe was turned into a disaster. The divisions of Victor and Oudinot—the last to preserve any semblance of military discipline—were almost annihilated. The French lost twelve thousand killed or drowned in the river, sixteen thousand prisoners, twelve of the remaining guns. But they were across the Bérésina. There was no longer a Grand Army, however. There was no army at all—only a starving, struggling trail of men stumbling through the snow, without organization or discipline or hope.

It was a disaster on the same gigantic scale as the past victories—a disaster worthy of such a conqueror. Even his enemies forgot to rejoice. They caught their breath and waited.

And suddenly came the news that Napoleon was in Paris.

CHAPTER XVII.

A FORLORN HOPE.

The fire i' the flint
Shows not, till it be struck.

"IT is time to do something," said Papa Barlasch on the December morning when the news reached Dantzig that Napoleon was no longer with the army—that he had made over the parody of command of the phantom army to Murat, King of Naples—that he had passed like an evil spirit unknown through Poland, Prussia, Germany, travelling twelve hundred miles night and day at breakneck speed, alone, racing to Paris to save his throne.

"It is time to do something," said all Europe, when it was too late. For Napoleon was himself again—alert, indomitable, raising a new army, calling on France to rise to such heights of energy and vitality as only France can compass; for the colder nations of the North lack the imagination that enables men to pit themselves against the gods at the bidding of some stupendous will, only second to the will of God Himself.

"Go to Dantzig, and hold it till I come," Napoleon had said to Rapp. "Retreat to Poland, and hold on to anything you can till I come back with a new army," he had commanded Murat and Prince Eugene.

"It is time to do something," said all the conquered nations, looking at each other for initiation. And lo! the Master of Surprises struck them dumb by his sudden apparition in his own capital, with all the strings of the European net gathered as if by magic into his own hands again.

While everybody told his neighbour that it was time to do something, no one knew what to do. For it has pleased the Creator to put a great many talkers into this world and only a few men of action to make its history.

Papa Barlasch knew what to do, however.

"Where is that sailor?" he asked Désirée, when she had told him the news which Mathilde brought in from the streets. "He who took the patron's valise that night—the cousin of your husband."

"There is a man at Zoppot who will tell you," she answered.

"Then I go to Zoppot."

Barlasch had lived unmolested in the Frauengasse since his return. He was an old man, ill-clad, with a bloody handkerchief bound over one eye. No one asked him any questions, except Sebastian, who heard again and again the tale of Moscow—how the army which had crossed into Russia four hundred thousand strong was reduced to a hundred thousand when the retreat began; how handmills were issued to the troops to grind corn which did not exist; how the horses died in thousands and the men in hundreds from starvation; how God at last had turned his face from Napoleon.

"Something must be done. The patron will do nothing; he is in the clouds, he is dreaming dreams of a new France, that *bourgeois*. I am an old man. Yes, I will go to Zoppot."

"You mean that we should have heard from Charles before now," said Désirée.

"Name of thunder! he may be in Paris!" exclaimed Barlasch, with the sudden anger that anxiety commands. "He is on the staff, I tell you."

For suspense is one of the most contagious of human emotions, and makes a quicker call upon our sympathy than any other. Do we not feel such a desire that our neighbour may know the worst without delay, that we race to impart it to him?

Nor was Désirée alone in the trial which had drawn certain lines about her gay lips; for Mathilde had told her father and sister that should Colonel de Casimir return from the war he would ask her hand in marriage.

"And that other—the Colonel," added Barlasch, glancing at Mathilde, "he is on the staff too. They are safe enough, I tell you that. They are doubtless together. They were together at Moscow. I saw them, and took an order from them. They were . . . at their work"

Mathilde did not like Papa Barlasch. She would, it seemed, rather have no news at all of de Casimir than learn it from the old soldier, for she quitted the room without even troubling to throw him a glance of disdain.

Barlasch waited with working lips until the sound of her footsteps ceased on the stairs. Then he pushed across the kitchen table a piece of writing-paper, rather yellow and woolly. It had been to Moscow and back.

"Write a word to him," he said. "I will take it to Zoppot."

"But you can send a message by the fisherman whose name I have given you," answered Désirée.

"And will he heed the message? Will he come ashore at a word from me—only Barlasch? Remember it is his life that he carries in his hand. An English sailor with a French name! Thunder of thunder! They would shoot him like a rat!"

Désirée shook her head; but Barlasch was not to be denied. He brought pen and ink from the dresser, and pushed them across the table.

"I would not ask it," he said, "if it was not necessary. Do you think he will mind the danger? He will like it. He will say to me, 'Barlasch, I thank you' Ah! I know him. Write. He will come."

"Why?" asked Désirée.

"Why? How should I know that? He came before when you asked him."

Désirée leant over the table and wrote six words:

"Come, if you can come safely."

Barlasch took up the paper, and, pushing up the bandage which had served to bring him unharmed through Russia, he frowned at it without understanding.

"It is not all writings that I can read," he admitted. "Have you signed it?"

"No."

"Then sign something that he will know, and no other—they might shoot me. Your baptismal name."

And she wrote "Désirée" after the six words.

Barlasch folded the paper carefully and placed it in the lining of an old felt hat of Sebastian's which he now wore. He bound a scarf over his ears, after the manner of those who live on the Baltic shores in winter.

"You can leave the rest to me," he said; and, with a nod and a grimace expressive of cunning, he left her.

He did not return that night. The days were short now, for the winter was well set in. It was nearly dark the next afternoon and very cold when he came back. He sent Lisa upstairs for Désirée.

"First," he said, "there is a question for the patron. Will he quit Dantzig?—that is the question."

"No," answered Désirée.

"Rapp is coming," said Barlasch, emphasizing each point with one finger against the side of his nose. "He will hold Dantzig. There will be a siege. Let the patron make no mistake. It will not be like the last one. Rapp was outside then; he will be inside this time. He will hold Dantzig till the bottom falls out of the world."

"My father will not leave," said Désirée. "He has said so. He knows that Rapp is coming, with the Russians behind him."

"But," interrupted Barlasch, "he thinks that Prussia will turn and declare war against Napoleon. That may be. Who knows? The question is, Can the patron be induced to quit Dantzig?"

Désirée shook her head.

"It is not I," said Barlasch, "who ask the question. You understand?"

"Yes, I understand. My father will not quit Dantzig."

Whereupon Barlasch made a gesture conveying a desire to think as kindly of Antoine Sebastian as he could.

"In half an hour," he said, when it is dark, will you come for a walk with me along the Langfuhr road—where the unfinished ramparts are ?"

Désirée looked at him and hesitated.

"Oh—good—if you are afraid——" said Barlasch.

"I am not afraid—I will come," she answered quickly.

The snow was hard when they set out, and squeaked under their feet, as it does with a low thermometer.

"We shall leave no tracks," said Barlasch, as he led the way off the Langfuhr road towards the river. There was broken ground here, where earthworks had been begun and never completed. The trees had been partly cut, and beneath the snow were square mounds showing where the timber had been piled up. But since the departure of Rapp, all had been left incomplete.

Barlasch turned towards Désirée and pointed out a rising knoll of land with fir-trees on it—an outline against the sky where a faint aurora borealis lit the north. She understood that Louis was waiting there, and must necessarily see them approaching across the untrodden snow. For an instant she lingered, and Barlasch turning, glanced at her sharply over his shoulder. She had come against her will, and her companion knew it. Her feet were heavy with misgiving, like the feet of one who treads an uncertain road into a strange country. She had been afraid of

Louis d'Arragon when she first caught sight of him in the Frauengasse. The fear of him was with her now, and would not depart until he himself swept it away by the first word he spoke.

He came out from beneath the trees, made a few steps forward, and then stopped. Again Désirée lingered, and Barlasch, who was naturally impatient, turned and took her by the arm.

"Is it the snow—that you find slippery?" he asked, not requiring an answer. A moment later Louis came forward.

"There is nothing but bad news," he said laconically. "Barlasch will have told you; but there is no need to give up hope. The army has reached the Niemen; the rearguard has quitted Vilna. There is nothing for it but to go and look for him."

"Who will go?" she asked quietly.

" I."

He was looking at her with grave eyes trained to darkness. But she looked past him towards the sky, which was faintly lighted by the aurora. Her averted eyes and rigid attitude were not without some suggestion of guilt.

"My ship is ice-bound at Reval," said D'Arragon, in a matter-of-fact way. "They have no use for me until the winter is over, and they have given me three months' leave."

"To go to England?" she asked.

"To go anywhere I like," he said, with a short laugh. "So I am going to look for Charles, and Barlasch will come with me."

"At a price," put in that soldier, in a shrewd undertone. "At a price."

"A small one," corrected Louis, turning to look at him with the close attention of one exploring a new country.

"Bah! You give what you can. One does not go back across the Niemen for pleasure. We bargained, and we came to terms. I got as much as I could."

Louis laughed, as if this were the blunt truth.

"If I had more, I would give you more. It is the money I placed in a Dantzig bank for my cousin. I must take it out again, that is all."

The last words were addressed to Désirée, as if he had acted in assurance of her approval.

"But I have more," she said; "a little—not very much. We must not think of money. We must do everything to find him—to give him help, if he needs it."

"Yes," answered Louis, as if she had asked him a question. "We must do everything; but I have no more money."

"And I have none with me. I have nothing that I can sell."

She withdrew her fur mitten and held out her hand, as if to show that she had no rings, except the plain gold one on her third finger.

"You have the ikon I brought you from Moscow," said Barlasch gruffly. "Sell that."

"No," answered Désirée; "I will not sell that."

Barlasch laughed cynically.

"There you have a woman," he said, turning to Louis. "First she will not have a thing, then she will not part with it."

"Well," said Désirée, with some spirit, "a woman may know her own mind."

"Some do," admitted Barlasch carelessly; "the happy ones. And since you will not sell your ikon, I must go for what Monsieur le capitaine offers me."

"Five hundred francs," said Louis. "A thousand francs, if we succeed in bringing my cousin safely back to Dantzig."

"It is agreed," said Barlasch, and Désirée looked from one to the other with an odd smile of amusement. For women do not understand that spirit of adventure which makes the mercenary soldier, and urges the sailor to join an exploring expedition without hope of any reward beyond his daily pay, for which he is content to work and die loyally.

"And I," she asked, "what am I to do?"

"We must know where to find you," replied D'Arragon.

There was so much in the simple answer that Désirée fell into a train of thought. It did not seem much for her to do, and yet it was all. For it summed up in six words a woman's life: to wait till she is found.

"I shall wait in Dantzig," she said at length.

Barlasch held up his finger close to her face so that she could not fail to see it, and shook it slowly from side to side commanding her careful and entire attention.

"And buy salt," he said. "Fill a cupboard full of salt. It is cheap enough in Dantzig now. The patron will not think of it. He is a dreamer. But a dreamer awakes at length, and is hungry. It is I who tell you—Barlasch."

He emphasized himself with a touch of his curved fingers on either shoulder.

"Buy salt," he said, and walked away to a rising knoll to make sure that no one was approaching. The moon was just below the horizon, and a yellow glow was already in the sky.

Désirée and Louis were left alone. He was looking at her, but she was watching Barlasch with a still persistency.

"He said that it is the happy women who know their own minds," she said slowly.

"I suppose he meant——Duty," she added at length, when Louis made no sign of answering.

"Yes," he said.

Barlasch was beckoning to her. She moved away, but stopped a few yards off, and looked at Louis again.

"Do you think it is any good trying?" she asked with a short laugh.

"It is no good trying unless you mean to succeed," he answered lightly. She laughed a second time and lingered, though Barlasch was calling her to come.

"Oh," she said, "I am not afraid of you when you say things like that. It is what you leave unsaid. I am afraid of you, I think, because you expect so much."

She tried to see his face.

"I am only an ordinary human being, you know," she said warningly.

Then she followed Barlasch.

CHAPTER XVIII.

MISSING.

I should fear those that dance before me now
Would one day stamp upon me; it has been done:
Men shut their doors against a setting sun

DURING the first weeks of December the biting wind abated for a time, and immediately the snow came. It fell for days, until at length the grey sky seemed exhausted; for the flakes sailed downwards in twos and threes like the stragglers of an army bringing up the rear. Then the sun broke through again, and all the world was a dazzling white.

There had been a cessation in that stream of pitiable men who staggered across the bridge from the Königsberg road. Some instinct had turned it southwards. Now it began again, and the rumour spread throughout the city that Rapp was coming. At length, in the middle of December, an officer brought word that Rapp with his staff would arrive next day.

Désirée heard the news without comment.

"You do not believe it?" asked Mathilde, who had come in with shining eyes and a pale face.

"Oh yes, I believe it."

"Then you forget," persisted Mathilde, "that Charles is on the staff. They may arrive to-night."

While they were speaking Sebastian came in. He looked quickly from one to the other.

"You have heard the news?" he asked.

"That the General is coming back?" said Mathilde.

"No; not that. Though it is true. Macdonald is in full retreat on Dantzig. The Prussians have abandoned him—at last."

He gave a queer laugh and stood looking towards the window with restless eyes that flitted from one object to another, as if he were endeavouring to follow in mind the quick course of events. Then he remembered Désirée and turned towards her.

"Rapp returns to-morrow," he said. "We may presume that Charles is with him."

"Yes," said Désirée, in a lifeless voice.

Sebastian wrinkled his eyes and gave an apologetic laugh.

"We cannot offer him a fitting welcome," he said, with a gesture of frustrated hospitality. "We must do what we can. You and he may, of course, consider this your home as long as it pleases you to remain with us. Mathilde, you will see that we have such delicacies in the house as Dantzig can now afford— and you, Désirée, will of course make such preparations as are necessary. It is well to remember, he may return . . . to-night."

Désirée went towards the door while Mathilde laid aside the delicate needlework which seemed to absorb her mind and employ her fingers from morning till night. She made a movement as if to accompany her sister, but Désirée shook her head sharply and Mathilde remained where she was, leaving Désirée to go upstairs alone.

The day was already drawing to its long twilight, and at four o'clock the night came. Sebastian went out as usual, though he had caught cold. But Mathilde stayed at home. Désirée sent Lisa to the shops in the Langenmarkt, which is the centre of business and gossip in Dantzig. Lisa always brought home the latest news. Mathilde came to the kitchen to seek something when the messenger returned. She heard Lisa tell Désirée that a few more stragglers had come in, but they brought no news of the General. The house seemed lonely now that Barlasch was gone.

Throughout the night the sound of sleigh-bells could be faintly heard through the double windows, though no sleigh passed through the Frauengasse. A hundred times the bells seemed to come closer, and always Désirée was ready behind the curtains to see the light flash past into the Pfaffengasse. With a shiver of suspense she crept back to bed to await the next alarm. In the early morning, long before it was light, the dull thud of steps on the trodden snow called her to the window again. She caught her breath as she drew back the curtain; for through the long watches of the night she had imagined every possible form of return.

This must be Barlasch. Louis and Barlasch must, of course, have met Rapp on his homeward journey. On finding Charles, they had sent Barlasch back in advance to announce the safety of Désirée's husband. Louis would, of course, not come to Dantzig. He would go north to Russia, to Reval, and perhaps home to England—never to return.

But it was not Barlasch. It was a woman who staggered past under a burden of firewood which she had collected in the woods of Schottland, and did not dare to carry through the streets by day.

At last the clocks struck six, and, soon after, Lisa's heavy footstep made the stairs creak and crack.

Désirée went downstairs before daylight. She could hear Mathilde astir in her room, and the light of candles was visible under her door. Désirée busied herself with household affairs.

"I have not slept," said Lisa bluntly, "for thinking that your husband might return, and fearing that we should make him wait in the street. But without doubt you would have heard him."

"Yes, I should have heard him."

"If it had been my husband, I should have been at the window all night," said Lisa, with a gay laugh—and Désirée laughed too.

Mathilde seemed a long time in coming, and when at length she appeared Désirée could scarcely repress a movement of surprise. Mathilde was dressed, all in her best, as for a *fête*

At breakfast Lisa brought the news told to her at the door that the Governor would re-enter the city in state with his staff at midday. The citizens were invited to decorate their streets, and to gather there to welcome the returning garrison.

"And the citizens will accept the invitation," commented Sebastian, with a curt laugh. "All the world has sneered at Russia since the Empire existed —and yet it has to learn from Moscow what part a citizen may play in war. These good Dantzigers will accept the invitation."

And he was right. For one reason or another the city did honour to Rapp. Even the Poles must have known by now that France had made tools of them. But as yet they could not realize that Napoleon had fallen. There were doubtless many spies in the streets that cold December day—one who listened for Napoleon; and another, peeping to this side and that, for the King of Prussia. Sweden also would need to know what Dantzig thought, and Russia must not be ignorant of the gossip in a great Baltic port.

Enveloped in their stiff sheepskins, concealed by the high collars which reached to the brim of their hats—showing nothing but eyes where the rime made old faces and young all alike, it was difficult for any to judge of his neighbour—whether he were Pole or Prussian, Dantziger or Swede. The women in thick shawls, with hoods or scarves concealing their faces, stood silently beside their husbands. It was only the children who asked a thousand questions, and got never an answer from the cautious descendants of a Hanseatic people.

"Is it the French or the Russians that are coming?" asked a child near to Désirée.

"Both," was the answer.

"But which will come first?"

"Wait and see—silentium," replied the careful Dantziger, looking over his shoulder.

Désirée had changed her clothes, and wore beneath her furs the dress that had been prepared for the journey to Zoppot so long ago. Mathilde had noticed the dress, which had not been seen for six months. Lisa, more loquacious, nodded to it as to a friend when helping Désirée with her furs.

"You have changed," she said, "since you last wore it."

P

"I have grown older—and fatter," answered Désirée cheerfully.

And Lisa, who had no imagination, seemed satisfied with the explanation. But the change was in Désirée's eyes.

With Sebastian's permission — almost at his suggestion—they had selected the Grüne Brucke as the point from which to see the sight. This bridge spans the Mottlau at the entrance to the Langenmarkt, and the roadway widens before it narrows again to pass beneath the Grunes Thor. There is rising ground where the road spreads like a fan, and here they could see and be seen.

"Let us hope," said Sebastian, "that two of these gentlemen may perceive you as they pass."

But he did not offer to accompany them.

By half-past eleven the streets were full. The citizens knew their governor, it seemed. He would not keep them waiting. Although Rapp lacked that power of appealing to the imagination which has survived Napoleon's death with such astounding vitality that it moves men's minds to-day as surely as it did a hundred years ago, he was shrewd enough to make use of his master's methods when such would seem to serve his purpose. He was not going to creep into Dantzig like a whipped dog into his kennel.

He had procured a horse at Elbing. Between that

town and the Mottlau he had halted to form his army into something like order, to get together a staff with which to surround himself.

But the Dantzigers did not cheer. They stood and watched him in a sullen silence as he rode across the bridge now known as the "Milk-Can." His bridle was twisted round his arm, for all his fingers were frostbitten. His nose and his ears were in the same plight, and had been treated by a Polish barber who, indeed, effected a cure. One eye was almost closed. His face was astonishingly red. But he carried himself like a soldier, and faced the world with the audacity that Napoleon taught to all his disciples.

Behind him rode a few staff officers, but the majority were on foot. Some effort had been made to revive the faded uniforms. One or two heroic souls had cast aside the fur cloaks to which they owed their life, but the majority were broken men without spirit, without pride—appealing only to pity. They hugged themselves closely in their ragged cloaks and stumbled as they walked. It was impossible to distinguish between the officers and the men. The biggest and the strongest were the best clad—the bullies were the best fed. All were black and smoke-grimed—with eyes reddened and inflamed by the dazzling snow through which they stumbled by day, as much as by the smoke into which they crouched at night. Every garment was riddled by the holes burnt by flying sparks—every face was smeared with blood that ran from the horseflesh they had torn asunder with their teeth while it yet smoked.

Some laughed and waved their hands to the crowd. Others, who had known the tragedy of Vilna and Kowno, stumbled on in stubborn silence still doubting that Dantzig stood—that they were at last in sight of food and warmth and rest.

"Is that all?" men asked each other in astonishment. For the last stragglers had crossed the new Mottlau before the head of the procession had reached the Grüne Brücke.

"If I had such an army as that," said a stout Dantziger, "I should bring it into the city quietly, after dusk."

But the majority were silent, remembering the departure of these men—the triumph, the glory, and the hope. For a great catastrophe is a curtain that for a moment shuts out all history and makes the human family little children again who can but cower and hold each other's hands in the dark.

"Where are the guns?" asked one.

"And the baggage?" suggested another.

"And the treasure of Moscow?" whispered a Jew with cunning eyes, who had hidden behind his neighbour when Rapp glanced in his direction.

Emerging on the bridge, the General glanced at

the old Mottlau. A crowd was collected on it. The citizens no longer used the bridges but crossed without fear where they pleased, and heavy sleighs passed up and down as on a high-road. Rapp saw it, made a grimace, and, turning in his saddle, spoke to his neighbour, an engineer officer, who was to make an immortal name and die in Dantzig.

The Mottlau was one of the chief defences of the city, but instead of a river the Governor found a high-road!

Rapp alone seemed to look about him with the air of one who knew his whereabouts. In the straggling trail of men behind him, not one in a hundred looked for a friendly face. Some stared in front of them with lifeless eyes, while others, with a little spirit plucked up at the end of a weary march, glanced up at the gabled houses with the interest called forth by the first sight of a new city.

It was not until long afterwards that the world, piecing together information purposely delayed and details carefully falsified, knew that of the four hundred thousand men who marched triumphantly to the Niemen, only twenty thousand recrossed that river six months later, and of these two-thirds had never seen Moscow.

Rapp, whose bloodshot eyes searched the crowd of faces turned towards him, recognized a number of people. To Mathilde he bowed gravely, and with a kindlier glance turned in his saddle to bow again to

Désirée. They hardly heeded him, but with colourless faces turned towards the staff riding behind him.

Most of the faces were strange: others were so altered that the features had to be sought for as in the face of a mummy. Neither Charles nor de Casimir was among the horsemen. One or two of them bowed, as their leader had done, to the two girls.

"That is Captain de Villars," said Mathilde, "and the other I do not know. Nor that tall man who is bowing now. Who are they?"

Désirée did not answer. None of these men was Charles. Unconsciously holding her two mittened hands at her throat, she searched each face.

They were well placed to see even those who followed on foot. Many of them were not French. It would have been easy to distinguish Charles or de Casimir among the dark-visaged southerners. Désirée was not conscious of the crowd around her. She heard none of the muttered remarks. All her soul was in her eyes.

"Is that all?" she said at length—as the others had said at the entrance to the town.

She found she was standing hand-in-hand with Mathilde, whose face was like marble.

At last, when even the crowd had passed away beneath the Grünes Thor, they turned and walked home in silence.

CHAPTER XIX.

KOWNO.

Distinct with footprints yet
Of many a mighty marcher gone that way.

THERE are many who overlook the fact that in Northern lands, more especially in such plains as Lithuania, Courland, and Poland, travel in winter is easier than at any other time of year. The rivers, which run sluggishly in their ditch-like beds, are frozen so completely that the bridges are no longer required. The roads, in summer almost impassable—mere ruts across the plain—are for the time ignored, and the traveller strikes a bee-line from place to place across a level of frozen snow.

Louis d'Arragon had worked out a route across the plain, as he had been taught to shape a course across a chart.

"How did you return from Kowno?" he asked Barlasch.

"Name of my own nose," replied that traveller. "I followed the line of dead horses."

"Then I will take you by another route," replied the sailor.

And three days later—before General Rapp had made his entry into Dantzig—Barlasch sold two skeletons of horses and a sleigh at an enormous profit to a staff-officer of Murat's at Gumbinnen.

They had passed through Rapp's army. They had halted at Königsberg to make inquiry, and now, almost in sight of the Niemen, where the land begins to heave in great waves, like those that roll round Cape Horn, they were asking still if any man had seen Charles Darragon.

"Where are you going, comrades?" a hundred men had paused to ask them.

"To seek a brother," answered Barlasch, who, like many unprincipled persons, had soon found that a lie is much simpler than an explanation.

But the majority glanced at them stupidly without comment, or with only a shrug of their bowed shoulders. They were going the wrong way. They must be mad. Between Dantzig and Königsberg they had indeed found a few travellers going eastward—despatch-bearers seeking Murat—spies going northwards to Tilsit, and General Yorck still in treaty with his own conscience—a prominent member of the Tugendbund, wondering, like many others, if there were any virtue left in the world. Others, again, told them that they weie officers ordered to take up some new command in the retreating army.

Beyond Königsberg, however, D'Arragon and Barlasch found themselves alone on their eastward route. Every man's face was set towards the west. This was not an army at all, but an endless procession of tramps. Without food or shelter, with no baggage but what they could carry on their backs, they journeyed as each of us must journey out of this world into that which lies beyond—alone, with no comrade to help them over the rough places or lift them when they fell. For there was only one man of all this rabble who rose to the height of self-sacrifice, and a persistent devotion to duty. And he was coming last of all.

Many had started off in couples—with a faithful friend—only to quarrel at last. For it is a peculiarity of the French that they can only have one friend at a time. Long ago—back beyond the Niemen—all friendships had been dissolved, and discipline had vanished before that. For when Discipline and a Republic are wedded we shall have the millennium. Liberty, they cry: meaning, I may do as I like. Equality: I am better than you. Fraternity: what is yours is mine, if I want it.

So they quarrelled over everything, and fought for a place round the fire that another had lighted. They burnt the houses in which they had passed a night, though they knew that thousands trudging behind them must die for lack of this poor shelter.

At the Bérésina they had fought on the bridge like wild animals, and those who had horses trod their comrades underfoot, or pushed them over the parapet. Twelve thousand perished on the banks or in the river, and sixteen thousand were left behind to the mercy of the Cossacks.

At Vilna the people were terrified at the sight of this inhuman rabble, which had commanded their admiration on the outward march. And the commander, with his staff, crept out of the city at night, abandoning sick, wounded, and fighting men.

At Kowno they crowded numbly across the bridge, fighting for precedence, when they might have walked at leisure across the ice. They were no longer men at all, but dumb and driven animals, who fell by the roadside, and were stripped by their comrades before the warmth of life had left their limbs.

"Excuse me, comrade? I thought you were dead," said one, on being remonstrated with by a dying man. And he went on his way reluctantly, for he knew that in a few minutes another would snatch the booty. But for the most part they were not so scrupulous.

At first D'Arragon, to whom these horrors were new, attempted to help such as appealed to him, but Barlasch laughed at him.

"Yes," he said. "Take the medallion, and promise to send it to his mother. Holy Heaven—they all have medallions, and they all have mothers. Every Frenchman remembers his mother—when it is too late. I will get a cart. By to-morrow we shall fill it with keepsakes. And here is another. He is hungry. So am I, comrade. I come from Moscow—bah!"

And so they fought their way through the stream. They could have journeyed by a quicker route—D'Arragon could have steered a course across the frozen plain as over a sea—but Charles must necessarily be in this stream. He might be by the wayside. Any one of these pitiable objects, half blind, frost-bitten, with one limb or another swinging useless, like a snapped branch, wrapped to the eyes in filthy furs—inhuman, horrible—any one of these might be Désirée's husband.

They never missed a chance of hearing news. Barlasch interrupted the last message of a dying man to inquire whether he had ever heard of Prince Eugene. It was startling to learn how little they knew. The majority of them were quite ignorant of French, and had scarcely heard the name of the commander of their division. Many spoke in a language which even Barlasch could not identify.

"His talk is like a coffee-mill," he explained to D'Arragon, "and I do not know to what regiment he belonged. He asked me if I was Russski—I! Then he wanted to hold my hand. And he went to sleep. He will wake among the angels—that parishioner."

Not only had no one heard of Charles Darragon, but few knew the name of the commander to whose staff he had been attached in Moscow. There was nothing for it but to go on towards Kowno, where it was understood temporary head-quarters had been established.

Rapp himself had told D'Arragon that officers had been despatched to Kowno to form a base—a sort of rock in the midst of a torrent to divert the currents. There had then been a talk of Tilsit, and diverting the stream, or part of it towards Macdonald in the north. But D'Arragon knew that Macdonald was likely to be in no better plight than Murat; for it was an open secret in Dantzig that Yorck, with four-fifths of Macdonald's army, was about to abandon him.

The road to Kowno was not to be mistaken. On either side of it, like fallen landmarks, the dead lay huddled on the snow. Sometimes D'Arragon and Barlasch found the remains of a fire, where, amid the ashes, the chains and rings showed that a gun-carriage had been burnt. The trees were cut and scored where, as a forlorn hope, some poor imbecile had stripped the bark with the thought that it might burn. Nearly every fire had its grim guardian; for the wounds of the injured nearly always mortified when the flesh was melted by the warmth. Once or twice, with their ragged feet in the ashes, a whole company had never awakened from their sleep.

Barlasch pessimistically went the round of these bivouacs, but rarely found anything worth carrying away. If he recognized a veteran by the grizzled hair straggling out of the rags in which all faces were enveloped, or perceived some remnant of a Garde uniform, he searched more carefully.

"There may be salt," he said. And sometimes he found a little. They had been on foot since Gumbinnen, because no horse would be allowed by starving men to live a day. They existed from day to day on what they found, which was, at the best, frozen horse. But Barlasch ate singularly little.

"One thinks of one's digestion," he said vaguely, and persuaded D'Arragon to eat his portion because it would be a sin to throw it away.

At length D'Arragon, who was quick enough in understanding rough men, said—

"No, I don't want any more. I will throw it away."

And an hour later, while pretending to be asleep, he saw Barlasch get up, and crawl cautiously into the trees where the unsavoury food had been thrown.

"Provided," muttered Barlasch one day, "that you keep your health. I am an old man. I could not do this alone."

Which was true, for D'Arragon was carrying all the baggage now.

"We must both keep our health," answered Louis. "I have eaten worse things than horse."

"I saw one yesterday," said Barlasch, with a gesture of disgust; "he had three stripes on his arm, too; he was crouching in a ditch eating something much worse than horse, mon capitaine. Bah! It made me sick. For three sous I would have put my heel on his face. And later on at the roadside I saw where he or another had played the butcher. But you saw none of these things, mon capitaine?"

"It was by that winding stream where a farm had been burnt," said Louis.

Barlasch glanced at him sideways.

"If we should come to that, mon capitaine. . . ."

"We won't."

They trudged on in silence for some time. They were off the road now, and D'Arragon was steering by dead-reckoning. Even amid the pine-woods, which seemed interminable, they frequently found remains of an encampment. As often as not they found the campers huddled over their last bivouac.

"But these," said Barlasch, pointing to what looked like a few bundles of old clothes, continuing the conversation where he had left it after a long silence, as men learn to do who are together day and night in some hard enterprise, "even these have a woman dinning the ears of the good God for them, just as we have."

For Barlasch's conception of a Deity could not get farther than the picture of a great Commander who in times of stress had no leisure to see that non-commissioned officers did their best for the rank and file. Indeed, the poor in all lands rather naturally conclude that God will think of carriage-people first.

They came within sight of Kowno one evening, after a tiring day over snow that glittered in a cloudless sun. Barlasch sat down wearily against a pine-tree, when they first caught sight of a distant church-tower. The country is much broken up into little valleys here, through which streams find their way to the Niemen. Each river necessitated a rapid descent and an arduous climb over slippery snow.

"Voilà," said Barlasch. "That is Kowno. I am done. Go on, mon capitaine. I will lie here, and if I am not dead to-morrow morning, I will join you."

Louis looked at him with a slow smile.

"I am tired as you," he said. "We will rest here until the moon rises."

Already the bare larches threw shadows three times their own length on the snow. Near at hand it glittered like a carpet of diamonds, while the distance was of a pale blue, merging to grey on the horizon. A

far-off belt of pines against a sky absolutely cloudless suggested infinite space—immeasurable distance.
Nothing was sharp and clearly outlined, but hazy,
silvery, as seen through a thin veil. The sea would
seem to be our earthly picture of infinite space, but no
sea speaks of distance so clearly as the plain of
Lithuania—absolutely flat, quite lonely. The far-off
belt of pines only leads the eye to a shadow beyond,
which is another pine-wood, and the traveller walking
all day towards it knows that when at length he gets
there he will see just such another on the far horizon.

Louis sat down wearily beside Barlasch. As far as
eye could see, they were alone in this grim white world.
They had nothing to say to each other. They sat and
watched the sun go down with drawn eyes and a queer
stolidity which comes to men in great cold, as if their
souls were numb.

As the sun sank, the shadows turned bluer, and all
the snow gleamed like a lake. The silver tints slowly
turned to gold; the greys grew darker. The distant
lines of pines were almost black now, a silhouette
against the golden sky. Near at hand the little in-
equalities in the snow loomed blue, like deeper pools
in shallow water.

The sun sank very slowly, moving along the horizon
almost parallel with it towards two bars of golden
cloud awaiting it, the bars of the West forming a

prison to this poor pale captive of the snows. The stems of a few silver-birch near at hand were rosy now, and suddenly the snow took a similar tint. At the same moment, a wave of cold seemed to sweep across the world.

The sun went down at length, leaving a brownish-red sky. This, too, faded to grey in a few minutes, and a steely cold gripped the world as in a vice.

Louis d'Arragon made a sudden effort and rose to his feet, beneath which the snow squeaked.

"Come," he said. "If we stay, we shall fall asleep, and then——"

Barlasch roused himself and looked sleepily at his companion. He had a patch of blue on either cheek.

"Come!" shouted Louis, as if to a deaf man. "Let us go on to Kowno, and find out whether he is alive or dead."

CHAPTER XX.

DÉSIRÉE'S CHOICE.

Our wills and fates do so contrary run,
That our devices still are overthrown.
Our thoughts are ours, their ends none of our own.

RAPP found himself in a stronghold which was strong in theory only. For the frozen river formed the easiest possible approach, instead of an insuperable barrier to the enemy. He had an army which was a paper army only.

He had, according to official returns, thirty-five thousand men. In reality a bare eight thousand could be collected to show a face to the enemy. The rest were sick and wounded. There was no national spirit among these men; they hardly had a language in common. For they were men from Africa and Italy, from France, Germany, Poland, Spain, and Holland. The majority of them were recruits, raw and of poor physique. All were fugitives, flying before those dread Cossacks whose "hurrah! hurrah!"—the Arabic "kill! kill!"—haunted their fitful sleep at night. They came to Dantzig not to fight, but to lie down and rest. They were the last of the great army—the reinforcements dragged to the frontier which many of them had never crossed. For those who had been to Moscow were few and far between. The army of Moscow had perished at Malo-Jaroslavetz, at the Bérésina, in Smolensk and Vilna.

These fugitives had fled to Dantzig for safety; and Rapp in crossing the bridge had made a grimace, for he saw that there was no safety here.

The fortifications had been merely sketched out. The ditches were full of snow, the rivers were frozen. All work was at a standstill. Dantzig lay at the mercy of the first-comer.

In twenty-four hours every available smith was at work, forging ice-axes and picks. Rapp was going to cut the frozen Vistula and set the river free. The Dantzigers laughed aloud.

"It will freeze again in a night," they said. And it did. So Rapp set the ice-cutters to work again next day. He kept boats moving day and night in the water, which ran sluggish and thick, like porridge, with the desire to freeze and be still.

He ordered the engineers to set to work on the abandoned fortifications. But the ground was hard like granite, and the picks sprang back in the worker's grip, jarring his bones, and making not so much as a mark on the surface of the earth.

Again the Dantzigers laughed.

"It is frozen three feet down," they said.

The thermometer marked between twenty and thirty degrees of frost every night now. And it was only December—only the beginning of the winter. The Russians were at the Niemen, daily coming nearer. Dantzig was full of sick and wounded. The available troops were worn out, frost-bitten, desperate. There were only a few doctors, who were without medical stores; no meat, no vegetables, no spirits, no forage.

No wonder the Dantzigers laughed Rapp, who had to rely on Southerners to obey his orders— Italians, Africans, a few Frenchmen, men little used to cold and the hardships of a Northern winter—Rapp let them laugh. He was a medium-sized man, with a bullet-head and a round chubby face, a small nose, round eyes, and, if you please, side-whiskers.

Never for a moment did he admit that things looked black. He lit enormous bonfires, melted the frozen earth, and built the fortifications that had been planned.

"I took counsel," he said, long afterwards, "with two engineer officers whose devotion equalled their brilliancy — Colonel Richemont and General Campredon."

And the educated English gentleman of to-day will tell you quite gravely that there are no soldiers in the world like English soldiers, and no general in the world like the latest pet general of English journalism. There is, as a matter of fact, no more ignorant gentleman in the world than the educated English gentleman; and he will confess quite grandly, without any abatement of his public school and university conceit, that he knows nothing of Rapp, and never heard of such persons as Colonel Richemont and General Campredon.

The days were very short now, and it was dark when the sappers—whose business it was to keep the ice moving in the river at that spot where the Government building-yard abuts the river front to-day—were roused from their meditations by a shout on the farther bank.

They pushed their clumsy boat through the ice, and soon perceived against the snowy distance the outline of a man wrapped, swaddled, disguised in the heaped-up clothing so familar to Eastern Europe at this time. The joke of seeing a grave artilleryman clad in a lady's ermine cloak had long since lost its savour for those who dwelt near the Moscow road.

" Ah! comrade," said one of the boatmen, an Italian who spoke French and had learnt his seamanship on the Mediterranean, by whose waters he would never idle again. " Ah! you are from Moscow?"

" And you, countryman?" replied the new-comer, with a non-committing readiness, as he stumbled over the gunwale.

"And you—an old man?" remarked the Italian, with the easy frankness of Piedmont.

By way of reply, the new-comer held out one hand roughly swathed in cloth, and shook it from side to side slowly, taking exception to such personal matters on a short acquaintance.

"A week ago, when I quitted Dantzig on a mission to Kowno," he said, with a careless air, "one could cross the Vistula anywhere. I have been walking on the bank for half a league looking for a way across. One would think there is a General in Dantzig now."

"There is Rapp," replied the Italian, poling his boat through the floating ice.

"He will be glad to see me."

The Italian turned and looked over his shoulder. Then he gave a curt, derisive laugh.

"Barlasch—of the Old Guard!" explained the new-comer, with a careless air.

"Never heard of him."

Barlasch pushed up the bandage which he still wore over his left eye, in order to get a better sight of this phenomenal ignoramus, but he made no comment.

On landing he nodded curtly, at which the boatman made a quick gesture and spat.

"You have not the price of a glass in your purse, perhaps," he suggested.

Barlasch disappeared in the darkness without

deigning a reply. Half an hour later he was on the steps of Sebastian's house in the Frauengasse. On his way through the streets a hundred evidences of energy had caught his attention, for many of the houses were barricaded, and palisades were built at the end of the streets running down towards the river. The town was busy, and everywhere soldiers passed to and fro. Like Samuel, Barlasch heard the bleating of sheep and the lowing of oxen in his ears.

The houses in the Frauengasse were barricaded like others—many of the lower windows were built up. The door of No 36 was bolted, and through the shutters of the upper windows no glimmer of light penetrated to the outer darkness of the street. Barlasch knocked and waited. He thought he could hear surreptitious movements within the house. Again he knocked.

"Who is that?" asked Lisa just within, on the mat. She must have been there all the time.

"Barlasch," he replied. And the bolts which he, in his knowledge of such matters, himself had oiled, were quickly drawn.

Inside he found Lisa, and behind her Mathilde and Désirée.

"Where is the patron?" he asked, turning to bolt the door again.

"He is out, in the town," answered Désirée, in a strained voice. "Where are you from?"

"From Kowno?"

Barlasch looked from one face to the other. His own was burnt red, and the light of the lamp hanging over his head gleamed on the icicles suspended to his eyebrows and ragged whiskers. In the warmth of the house his frozen garments began to melt, and from his limbs the water dripped to the floor with a sound like rain. Then he caught sight of Désirée's face.

"He is alive, I tell you that," he said abruptly. "And well, so far as we know. It was at Kowno that we got news of him. I have a letter."

He opened his cloak, which was stiff like cardboard and creaked when he bent the rough cloth. Under his cloak he wore a Russian peasant's sheepskin coat, and beneath that the remains of his uniform.

"A dog's country," he muttered, as he breathed on his fingers.

At last he found the letter, and gave it to Désirée.

"You will have to make your choice," he commented, with a grimace indicative of a serious situation, "like any other woman. No doubt you will choose wrong."

Désirée went up two steps in order to be nearer the lamp, and they all watched her as she opened the letter.

"Is it from Charles?" asked Mathilde, speaking for the first time.

"No," answered Désirée, rather breathlessly.

Barlasch nudged Lisa, indicated his own mouth, and pushed her towards the kitchen. He nodded cunningly to Mathilde, as if to say that they were now free to discuss family affairs; and added, with a gesture towards his inner man—

"Since last night—nothing."

In a few minutes Désirée, having read the letter twice, handed it to her sister. It was characteristically short.

"We have found a man here," wrote Louis d'Arragon, "who travelled as far as Vilna with Charles. There they parted. Charles, who was ordered to Warsaw on staff work, told his friend that you were in Dantzig, and that, foreseeing a siege of the city, he had written to you to join him at Warsaw. This letter has doubtless been lost. I am following Charles to Warsaw, tracing him step by step, and if he has fallen ill by the way, as so many have done, shall certainly find him. Barlasch returns to bring you to Thorn, if you elect to join Charles. I will await you at Thorn, and if Charles has proceeded, we will follow him to Warsaw."

Barlasch, who had watched Désirée, now followed Mathilde's eyes as they passed to and fro over the closely written lines. As she neared the end, and her face, upon which deep shadows had been graven by sorrow and suspense, grew drawn and hopeless, he gave a curt laugh.

"There were two," he said, "travelling together—the Colonel de Casimir and the husband of—of la petite. They had facilities—name of God!—two carriages and an escort. In the carriages they had some of the Emperor's playthings—holy pictures, the imperial loot—I know not what. Besides that, they had some of their own—not furs and candlesticks such as we others carried on our backs, but gold and jewellery enough to make a man rich all his life.

"How do you know that?" asked Mathilde; a dull light in her eyes.

"I—I know where it came from," replied Barlasch, with an odd smile. "Allez! you may take it from me." And he muttered to himself in the patois of the Côtes du Nord.

"And they were safe and well at Vilna?" asked Mathilde.

"Yes—and they had their treasure. They had good fortune, or else they were more clever than other men; for they had the Imperial treasure to escort, and could take any man's horse for the carriages in which also they had placed their own treasure. It was Captain Darragon who held the appointment, and the other—the Colonel—had attached himself to him as volunteer. For it was at Vilna that the last thread of discipline was broken, and every man did as he wished."

"They did not come to Kowno?" asked Mathilde, who had a clear mind, and that grasp of a situation which more often falls to the lot of the duller sex.

"They did not come to Kowno. They would turn south at Vilna. It was as well. At Kowno the soldiers had broken into the magazines—the brandy was poured out in the streets. The men were lying there, the drunken and the dead all confused together on the snow. But there would be no confusion the next morning; for all would be dead."

"Was it at Kowno that you left Monsieur d'Arragon?" asked Désirée, in a sharp voice.

"No—no. We quitted Kowno together, and parted on the heights above the town. He would not trust me—monsieur le marquis—he was afraid that I should get at the brandy. And he was right. I only wanted the opportunity. He is a strong one—that!" And Barlasch held up a warning hand, as if to make known to all and sundry that it would be inadvisable to trifle with Louis d'Arragon.

He drew the icicles one by one from his whiskers with a wry face indicative of great agony, and threw them down on the mat.

"Well," he said, after a pause, to Désirée, "have you made your choice?"

Désirée was reading the letter again, and before she could answer, a quick knock on the front door startled them all. Barlasch's face broke into that broad smile which was only called forth by the presence of danger.

"Is it the patron?" he asked in a whisper, with his hand on the heavy bolts affixed by that pious Hanseatic merchant who held that if God be in the house there is no need of watchmen.

"Yes," answered Mathilde. "Open quickly."

Sebastian came in with a light step. He was like a man long saddled with a burden of which he had at length been relieved.

"Ah! What news?" he asked, when he recognised Barlasch.

"Nothing that you do not know already, monsieur," replied Barlasch, "except that the husband of Mademoiselle is well and on the road to Warsaw. Here—read that."

And he took the letter from Désirée's hand.

"I knew he would come back safely," said Désirée; and that was all.

Sebastian read the letter in one quick glance—and then fell to thinking.

"It is time to quit Dantzig," said Barlasch quietly, as if he had divined the old man's thoughts. "I know Rapp. There will be trouble—here, on the Vistula."

But Sebastian dismissed the suggestion with a curt shake of the head.

Barlasch's attention had been somewhat withdrawn by a smell of cooking meat, to which he opened his nostrils frankly and noisily after the manner of a dog.

"Then it remains," he said, looking towards the kitchen, "for Mademoiselle to make her choice."

"There is no choice," replied Désirée, "I shall be ready to go with you—when you have eaten."

"Good," said Barlasch, and the word applied as well to Lisa, who was beckoning to him.

CHAPTER XXI.

ON THE WARSAW ROAD.

Oft expectation fails, and most oft there
Where it most promises, and oft it hits
Where hope is coldest and despair most sits

LOVE, it is said, is blind. But hatred is as bad. In Antoine Sebastian hatred of Napoleon had not only blinded eyes far-seeing enough in earlier days, but it had killed many natural affections. Love, too, may easily die—from a surfeit or a famine. Hatred never dies; it only sleeps.

Sebastian's hatred was all awake now. It was aroused by the disasters that had befallen Napoleon; of which disasters the Russian campaign was only one small part. For he who stands above all his compeers must expect them to fall upon him should he stumble. Napoleon had fallen, and a hundred foes who had hitherto nursed their hatred in a hopeless silence were alert to strike a blow should he descend within their reach.

When whole empires had striven in vain to strike,

how could a mere association of obscure men hope to record its blow? The Tugendbund had begun humbly enough; and Napoleon, with that unerring foresight which raised him above all other men, had struck at its base. For an association in which kings and cobblers stand side by side on an equal footing must necessarily be dangerous to its foes.

Sebastian was not carried off his feet by the great events of the last six months. They only rendered him steadier. For he had waited a lifetime. It is only a sudden success that dazzles. Long waiting nearly always ensures a wise possession.

Sebastian, like all men absorbed in a great thought, was neglectful of his social and domestic obligations. Has it not been shown that he allowed Mathilde and Désirée to support him by giving dancing lessons? But he was not the ordinary domestic tyrant who is familiar to us all—the dignified father of a family who must have the best of everything, whose teaching to his offspring takes the form of an unconscious and solemn warning. He did not ask the best; he hardly noticed what was offered to him; and it was not owing to his demand, but to that feminine spirit of self-sacrifice which has ruined so many men, that he fared better than his daughters.

If he thought about it at all, he probably concluded that Mathilde and Désirée were quite content to give their time and thought to the support of himself—not as their father, but as the motive power of the Tugendbund in Prussia. Many greater men have made the same mistake, and quite small men with a great name make it every day, thinking complacently that it is a privilege to some woman to minister to their wants while they produce their immortal pictures or deathless books; whereas, the woman would tend him as carefully were he a crossing-sweeper, and is only following the dictates of an instinct which is loftier than his highest thought and more admirable than his most astounding work of art.

Barlasch had not lived so long in the Frauengasse without learning the domestic economy of Sebastian's household. He knew that Désirée, like many persons with kind blue eyes, shaped her own course through life, and abided by the result with a steadfastness not usually attributed to the light-hearted. He concluded that he must make ready to take the road again before midnight. He therefore gave a careful and businesslike attention to the simple meal set before him by Lisa; and, looking up over his plate, he saw for the second time in his life Sebastian hurrying into his own kitchen.

Barlasch half rose, and then, in obedience to a gesture from Sebastian, or remembering perhaps the sturdy Republicanism which he had not learnt until middle-age, he sat down again, fork in hand.

"You are prepared to accompany Madame Darragon to Thorn?" inquired Sebastian, inviting his guest by a gesture to make himself at home—scarcely a necessary thought in the present instance.

"Yes."

"And how do you propose to make the journey?"

This was so unlike Sebastian's usual method, so far from his lax comprehension of a father's duty, that Barlasch paused and looked at him with suspicion. With the back of his hand he pushed up the unkempt hair which obscured his eyes. This unusual display of parental anxiety required looking into.

"From what I could see in the streets," he answered, "the General will not stand in the way of women and useless mouths who wish to quit Dantzig."

"That is possible; but he will not go so far as to provide horses."

Barlasch gave his companion a quick glance, and returned to his supper, eating with an exaggerated nonchalance, as if he were alone.

"Will you provide them?" he asked abruptly, at length, without looking up.

"I can get them for you, and can ensure you relays by the way."

Barlasch cut a piece of meat very carefully, and, opening his mouth wide, looked at Sebastian over the orifice.

"On one condition," pursued Sebastian quietly; "that you deliver a letter for me in Thorn. I make no pretence; if it is found on you, you will be shot."

Barlasch smiled pleasantly.

"The risks are very great," said Sebastian, tapping his snuff-box reflectively.

"I am not an officer to talk of my honour," answered Barlasch, with a laugh. "And as for risk" —he paused and put half a potato into his mouth— "it is Mademoiselle I serve," concluded this uncouth knight with a curt simplicity.

So they set out at ten o'clock that night in a light sleigh on high runners, such as may be seen on any winter day in Poland down to the present time. The horses were as good as any in Dantzig at this date, when a horse was more costly than his master. The moon, sailing high overhead through fleecy clouds, found it no hard task to light a world all snow and ice. The streets of Dantzig were astir with life and the rumble of waggons. At first there were difficulties, and Barlasch explained airily that he was not so accomplished a whip in the streets as in the open country.

"But never fear," he added. "We shall get there, soon enough."

At the city gates there was, as Barlasch had predicted, no objection made to the departure of a young girl and an old man. Others were quitting Dantzig by the same gate, on foot, in sleighs and carts; but all turned westward at the cross-roads and joined the stream of refugees hurrying forward to Germany. Barlasch and Désirée were alone on the wide road that runs southward across the plain towards Dirschau. The air was very cold and still. On the snow, hard and dry like white dust, the runners of the sleigh sang a song on one note, only varied from time to time by a drop of several octaves as they passed over a culvert or some hollow in the road, after which the high note, like the sound of escaping steam, again held sway. The horses fell into a long steady trot, their feet beating the ground with a regular, sleep-inducing thud. They were harnessed well forward to a very long pole, and covered the ground with free strides, unhampered by any thought of their heels. The snow pattered against the cloth stretched like a wind-sail from their flanks to the rising front of the sleigh.

Barlasch sat upright, a thick motionless figure, four-square, to the cutting wind. He drove with one hand at a time, sitting on the other to restore circulation between whiles. It was impossible to distinguish the form of his garments, for he was wrapped round in a woollen shawl like a mummy, showing only his eyes beneath the ragged fur of a sheepskin cap upon which the rime caused by the warmth of the horses and his own breath had frozen like a coating of frosted silver.

Désirée was huddled down beside him, with her head bent forward so as to protect her face from the wind, which seared like a hot iron. She wore a hood of white fur lined with a darker fur, and when she lifted her face only her eyes, bright and wakeful, were visible.

"If you are warm, you may go to sleep," said Barlasch in a mumbling voice, for his face was drawn tight and his lips stiffened by the cold. "But if you shiver, you must stay awake."

But Désirée seemed to have no wish for sleep. Whenever Barlasch leant forward to peer beneath her hood she looked round at him with wakeful eyes. Whenever, to see if she were still awake, he gave her an unceremonious nudge, she nudged back again instantly. As the night wore on, she grew more wakeful. When they halted at a wayside inn, which must have been minutely described to Barlasch by Sebastian, and Désirée accepted the innkeeper's offer of a cup of coffee by the fire while fresh horses were being put into harness, she was wide awake and looked at Barlasch with a reckless laugh as he shook the rime

from his eyebrows. In response he frowningly scruti-
nized as much of her face as he could see, and shook
his head disapprovingly.

"You laugh when there is nothing to laugh at,"
he said grimly. "Foolish. It makes people wonder
what is in your mind."

"There is nothing in my mind," she answered
gaily.

"Then there is something in your heart, and that
is worse!" said Barlasch, which made Désirée look at
him doubtfully.

They had done forty miles with the same horses,
and were nearly halfway. For some hours the road
had followed the course of the Vistula on the high
tableland above the river, and would so continue until
they reached Thorn.

"You must sleep," said Barlasch curtly, when they
were once more on the road. She sat silent beside
him for an hour. The horses were fresh, and covered
the ground at a great pace. Barlasch was no driver,
but he was skilful with the horses, and husbanded
their strength at every hill.

"If we go on like this, when shall we arrive?"
asked Désirée suddenly.

"By eight o'clock, if all goes well."

"And we shall find Monsieur Louis d'Arragon
awaiting us at Thorn?"

Barlasch shrugged his shoulders doubtfully.

"He said he would be there," he muttered, and, turning in his seat, he looked down at her with some contempt.

"That is like a woman," he said. "They think all men are fools except one, and that one is only to be compared with the bon Dieu."

Désirée could not have heard the remark, for she made no answer and sat silent, leaning more and more heavily against her companion. He changed the reins to his other hand, and drove with it for an hour after all feeling had left it. Désirée was asleep. She was still sleeping when, in the dim light of a late dawn, Barlasch saw the distant tower of Thorn Cathedral.

They were no longer alone on the road now, but passed a number of heavy market-sleighs bringing produce and wood to the town. Barlasch had been in Thorn before. Désirée was still sleeping when he turned the horses into the crowded yard of the "Drei Kronen." The sleighs and carriages were packed side by side as in a warehouse, but the stables were empty. No eager host came out to meet the travellers. The innkeepers of Thorn had long ceased to give themselves that trouble. For the city was on the direct route of the retreat, and few who got so far had any money left.

Slowly and painfully Barlasch unwound himself

and disentangled his legs. He tried first one and then the other, as if uncertain whether he could walk. Then he staggered numbly across the yard to the door of the inn.

A few minutes later Désirée woke up. She was in a room warmed by a great white stove and dimly lighted by candles. Some one was pulling off her gloves and feeling her hands to make sure that they were not frost-bitten. She looked sleepily at a white coffee-pot standing on the table near the candles; then her eyes, still uncomprehending, rested on the face of the man who was loosening her hood, which was hard with rime and ice. He had his back to the candles, and was half-hidden by the collar of his fur coat, which met the cap pressed down over his ears.

He turned towards the table to lay aside her gloves, and the light fell on his face. Désirée was wideawake in an instant, and Louis d'Arragon, hearing her move, turned anxiously to look at her again. Neither spoke for a minute. Barlasch was holding his numbed hand against the stove, and was grinding his teeth and muttering at the pain of the restored circulation.

Désirée shook the icicles from her hood, and they rattled like hail on the bare floor. Her hair, all tumbled round her face, caught the light of the candles. Her eyes were bright and the colour was in her cheeks. D'Arragon glanced at her with a sudden look of relief, and then turned to Barlasch. He took the numbed hand and felt it; then he held a candle close to it. Two of the fingers were quite white, and Barlasch made a grimace when he saw them. D'Arragon began rubbing at once, taking no notice of his companion's moans and complaints.

Without desisting, he looked over his shoulder towards Désirée, but not actually at her face.

"I heard last night," he said, "that the two carriages are standing in an inn-yard three leagues beyond this on the Warsaw road. I have traced them step by step from Kowno. My informant tells me that the escort has deserted, and that the officer in charge, Colonel Darragon, was going on alone, with the two drivers, when he was taken ill. He is nearly well again, and hopes to continue his journey to-morrow or the next day."

Désirée nodded her head to signify that she had heard and understood. Barlasch gave a cry of pain, and withdrew his hand with a jerk.

"Enough, enough!" he said. "You hurt me. The life is returning now; a drop of brandy perhaps——"

"There is no brandy in Thorn," said D'Arragon, turning towards the table. "There is only coffee."

He busied himself with the cups, and did not look at Désirée when he spoke again.

"I have secured two horses," he said, "to enable

you to proceed at once, if you are able to. But if you would rather rest here to-day——"

"Let us go on at once," interrupted Désirée hastily.

Barlasch, crouching against the stove, glanced from one to the other beneath his heavy brows, wondering, perhaps, why they avoided looking at each other.

"You will wait here," said D'Arragon, turning towards him, "until—until I return."

"Yes," was the answer. "I will lie on the floor here and sleep. I have had enough. I——"

Louis left the room to give the necessary orders. When he returned in a few minutes, Barlasch was asleep on the floor, and Désirée had tied on her hood again, which concealed her face. He drank a cup of coffee and ate some dry bread absent-mindedly, in silence.

The sound of bells, feebly heard through the double windows, told them that the horses were being harnessed.

"Are you ready?" asked D'Arragon, who had not sat down; and in response, Désirée, standing near the stove, went towards the door, which he held open for her to pass out. As she passed him, she glanced at his face, and winced.

In the sleigh she looked up at him as if expecting him to speak. He was looking straight in front of him. There was, after all, nothing to be said. She could see his steady eyes between his high collar and the fur cap. They were hard and unflinching. The road was level now, and the snow beaten to a gleaming track like ice. D'Arragon put the horses to a gallop at the town gate, and kept them at it.

In half an hour he turned towards her and pointed with his whip to a roof half hidden by some thin pines.

"That is the inn," he said.

In the inn yard he indicated with his whip two travelling-carriages standing side by side.

"Colonel Darragon is here?" he said to the cringing Jew who came to meet them; and the innkeeper led the way upstairs. The house was a miserable one, evil-smelling, sordid. The Jew pointed to a door, and, cringing again, left them.

Désirée made a gesture telling Louis to go in first, which he did at once. The room was littered with trunks and cases. All the treasure had been brought into the sick man's chamber for greater safety.

On a narrow bed near the window a man lay huddled on his side. He turned and looked over his shoulder, showing a haggard face with a ten-days' beard on it. He looked from one to the other in silence.

It was Colonel de Casimir.

CHAPTER XXII.

THROUGH THE SHOALS.

I see my way, as birds their trackless way

DE CASIMIR had never seen Louis d'Arragon, and yet some dim resemblance to his cousin must have introduced the new-comer to a conscience not quite easy.

"You seek me, Monsieur," he asked, not having recognized Désirée, who stood behind her companion, in her furs.

"I seek Colonel Darragon, and was told that we should find him in this room."

"May I ask why you seek him in this rather unceremonious manner?" asked De Casimir, with the ready insolence of his calling and his age.

"Because I am his cousin," replied Louis quietly, "and Madame is his wife."

Désirée came forward, her face colourless. She caught her breath, but made no attempt to speak.

De Casimir tried to lift himself on his elbows.

"Ah! madame," he said. "You see me in a sorry state. I have been very ill." And he made a gesture with one hand, begging her to overlook his unkempt appearance and the disorder of his room

"Where is Charles?" asked Désirée curtly. She had suddenly realized how intensely she had always disliked De Casimir, and distrusted him.

"Has he not returned to Dantzig?" was the ready answer. "He should have been there a week ago. We parted at Vilna. He was exhausted—a mere question of over-fatigue—and at his request I left him there to recover and to pursue his way to Dantzig, where he knew you would be awaiting him."

He paused and looked from one to the other with quick and furtive eyes. He felt himself easily a match for them in quickness of perception, in rapid thought, in glib speech. Both were dumb—he could not guess why. But there was a steadiness in D'Arragon's eyes which rarely goes with dulness of wit. This was a man who could be quick at will—a man to be reckoned with.

"You are wondering why I travel under your cousin's name, Monsieur," said De Casimir, with a friendly smile.

"Yes," returned Louis, without returning the smile.

"It is simple enough," explained the sick man. "At Vilna we found all discipline relaxed There were no longer any regiments. There was no longer a staff. There was no longer an army. Every man did as he thought best. Many, as you know, elected to await the Russians at Vilna, rather than attempt to journey farther. Your cousin had been given the command of the escort which has now filtered away, like every other corps. He was to conduct back to Paris two carriages laden with imperial treasure and certain papers of value. Charles did not want to go back to Paris. He wished most naturally to return to Dantzig. I, on the other hand, desired to go to France; and there place my sword once more at the Emperor's service. What more simple than to change places?"

"And names," suggested D'Arragon, without falling into De Casimir's easy and friendly manner.

"For greater security in passing through Poland and across the frontier," explained De Casimir readily. "Once in France—and I hope to be there in a week— I shall report the matter to the Emperor as it really happened: namely, that, owing to Colonel Darragon's illness, he transferred his task to me at Vilna. The Emperor will be indifferent, so long as the order has been carried out."

De Casimir turned to Désirée as likely to be more responsive than this dark-eyed stranger, who listened with so disconcerting a lack of comment or sympathy.

"So you see, madame," he said, "Charles will still get the credit for having carried out his most difficult task, and no harm is done."

"When did you leave Charles at Vilna?" asked she.

De Casimir lay back on the pillow in an attitude which betrayed his weakness and exhaustion. He looked at the ceiling with lustreless eyes.

"It must have been a fortnight ago," he said at length. "I was trying to count the days. We have lost all account of dates since quitting Moscow. One day has been like another—and all, terrible. Believe me, madame, it has always been in my mind that you were awaiting the return of your husband at Dantzig. I spared him all I could. A dozen times we saved each other's lives."

In six words Désirée could have told him all she knew: that he was a spy who had betrayed to death and exile many Dantzigers whose hospitality had been extended to him as a Polish officer; that Charles was a traitor who had gained access to her father's house in order to watch him—though he had honestly fallen in love with her. He was in love with her still, and he was her husband. It was this thought that broke into her sleep at night, that haunted her waking hours.

She glanced at Louis d'Arragon, and held her peace.

"Then, Monsieur," he said, "you have every reason to suppose that if Madame returns to Dantzig now, she will find her husband there?"

De Casimir looked at D'Arragon, and hesitated for

an instant. They both remembered afterwards that moment of uncertainty.

"I have every reason to suppose it," replied De Casimir at length, speaking in a low voice, as if fearful of being overheard.

Louis waited a moment, and glanced at Désirée, who, however, had evidently nothing more to say.

"Then we will not trouble you farther," he said, going towards the door, which he held open for Désirée to pass out. He was following her when De Casimir called him back.

"Monsieur," cried the sick man, "Monsieur, one moment, if you can spare it."

Louis came back. They looked at each other in silence while they heard Désirée descend the stairs and speak in German to the innkeeper who had been waiting there.

"I will be quite frank with you," said De Casimir, in that voice of confidential friendliness which so rarely failed in its effect. "You know that Madame Darragon has an elder sister, Mademoiselle Mathilde Sebastian?"

"Yes."

De Casimir raised himself on his elbows again, with an effort, and gave a short, half shamefaced laugh which was quite genuine. It was odd that Mathilde and he, who had walked most circumspectly, should both have been tripped up, as it were, by love.

"Bah!" he said, with a gesture dismissing the subject, "I cannot tell you more. It is a woman's secret, Monsieur, not mine. Will you deliver a letter for me in Dantzig, that is all I ask?"

"I will give it to Madame Darragon to give to Mademoiselle Mathilde, if you like; I am not returning to Dantzig," replied Louis. But de Casimir shook his head.

"I am afraid that will not do," he said doubtfully. "Between sisters, you understand——"

And he was no doubt right; this man of quick perception. Is it not from our nearest relative that our dearest secret is usually withheld?

"You cannot find another messenger?" asked De Casimir, and the anxiety in his face was genuine enough.

"I can—if you wish it."

"Ah, Monsieur, I shall not forget it! I shall never forget it," said the sick man quickly and eagerly. "The letter is there, beneath that sabretasche. It is sealed and addressed."

Louis found the letter, and went towards the door, as he placed it in his pocket.

"Monsieur," said De Casimir, stopping him again. "Your name, if I may ask it, so that I may remember a countryman who has done me so great a service."

"I am not a countryman; I am an Englishman," replied Louis. "My name is Louis d'Arragon."

"Ah! I know. Charles has told me, Monsieur le——"

But D'Arragon heard no more, for he closed the door behind him.

He found Désirée awaiting him in the entrance hall of the inn, where a fire of pine-logs burnt in an open chimney. The walls and low ceiling were black with smoke, the little windows were covered with ice an inch thick. It was twilight in this quiet room, and would have been dark but for the leaping flames of the fire.

"You will go back to Dantzig," he asked, "at once?"

He carefully avoided looking at her, though he need not have feared that she would have allowed her eyes to meet his. And thus they stood, looking downward to the fire—alone in a world that heeded them not, and would forget them in a week—and made their choice of a life.

"Yes," she answered.

He stood thinking for a moment. He was quite practical and matter-of-fact; and had the air of a man of action rather than of one who deals in thoughts, and twists them hither and thither so that good is made to look ridiculous, and bad is tricked out with a fine new name. He frowned as he looked at the fire with eyes that flitted from one object to another,

S

as men's eyes do who think of action and not of thought. This was the sailor—second to none in the shallow northern sea, where all marks had been removed, and every light extinguished—accustomed to facing danger and avoiding it, to foresee remote contingencies and provide against them, day and night, week in, week out; a sailor, careful and intrepid. He had the air of being capable of that concentration without which no man can hope to steer a clear course at all.

"The horses that brought you from Marienwerder will not be fit for the road till to-morrow morning," he said. "I will take you back to Thorn at once, and—leave you there with Barlasch."

He glanced towards her, and she nodded, as if acknowledging the sureness and steadiness of the hand at the helm.

"You can start early to-morrow morning, and be in Dantzig to-morrow night."

They stood side by side in silence for some minutes. He was still thinking of her journey—of the dangers and the difficulties of that longer journey through life without landmark or light to guide her.

"And you?" she asked curtly.

He did not reply at once but busied himself with his ponderous fur coat, which he buttoned, as if bracing himself for the start. Beneath her lashes she looked sideways at the deliberate hands and the lean strong face, burnt to a red-brown by sun and snow, half hidden in the fur collar of his worn and weather-beaten coat.

"Königsberg," he answered, "and Riga."

A light passed through her watching eyes, usually so kind and gay; like the gleam of jealousy.

"Your ship?" she asked sharply.

"Yes," he answered, as the innkeeper came to tell them that their sleigh awaited them.

It was snowing now, and a whistling, fitful wind swept down the valley of the Vistula from Poland and the far Carpathians which made the travellers crouch low in the sleigh and rendered talk impossible, had there been anything to say. But there was nothing.

They found Barlasch asleep where they had left him in the inn at Thorn, on the floor against the stove. He roused himself with the quickness and complete-ness of one accustomed to brief and broken rest, and stood up shaking himself in his clothes, like a dog with a heavy coat He took no notice of D'Arragon, but looked at Désirée with questioning eyes.

"It was not the Captain?" he asked.

And Désirée shook her head. Louis was standing near the door giving orders to the landlady of the inn—a kindly Pomeranian, clean and slow—for Désirée's comfort till the next morning.

Barlasch went close to Désirée, and, nudging her arm with exaggerated cunning, whispered—

"Who was it?"

"Colonel de Casimir."

"With the two carriages and the treasure from Moscow?" asked Barlasch, watching Louis out of the corner of one eye, to make sure that he did not hear. It did not matter whether he heard or not, but Barlasch came of a peasant stock that always speaks of money in a whisper. And when Désirée nodded, he cut short the conversation.

The hostess came forward to tell Désirée that her room was ready, kindly suggesting that the "gnädiges Fraülein" must need sleep and rest. Désirée knew that Louis would go on to Königsberg at once. She wondered whether she should ever see him again— long afterwards, perhaps, when all this would seem like a dream. Barlasch, breathing noisily on his frost-bitten fingers, was watching them. Désirée shook hands with Louis in an odd silence, and, turning on her heel, followed the woman out of the room without looking back.

CHAPTER XXIII.

AGAINST THE STREAM.

Wo viel Licht ist, ist starker Schatten.

IN the mean time the last of the Great Army had reached the Niemen, that narrow winding river in its ditch-like bed sunk below the level of the tableland, to which six months earlier the greatest captain this world has ever seen rode alone, and, coming back to his officers, said—

"Here we cross."

Four hundred thousand men had crossed—a bare eighty thousand lived to pass the bridge again. Twelve hundred cannons had been left behind, nearly a thousand in the hands of the enemy, and the remainder buried or thrown into those dull rivers whose slow waters flow over them to this day. One hundred and twenty-five thousand officers and men had been killed in battle, another hundred thousand had perished by cold and disaster at the Bérésina or other rivers where panic seized the fugitives.

Forty-eight generals had been captured by the

Russians, three thousand officers, one hundred and ninety thousand men, swallowed by the silent white Empire of the North and no more seen.

As the retreat neared Vilna the cold had increased, killing men as the first cold of an English winter kills flies. And when the French quitted Vilna, the Russians were glad enough to seek its shelter, Kutusoff creeping in with forty thousand men, all that remained to him of two hundred thousand. He could not carry on the pursuit, but sent forward a handful of Cossacks to harry the hare-brained few who called themselves the rearguard. He was an old man, nearly worn out, with only three months more to live—but he had done his work.

Ney—the bravest of the brave—left alone in Russia at the last with seven hundred foreign recruits, men picked from here and there, called in from the highways and hedges to share the glory of the only Marshal who came back from Moscow with a name untarnished—Ney and Girard, musket in hand, were the last to cross the bridge, shouting defiance at their Cossack foes, who, when they had hounded the last of the French across the frontier, flung themselves down on the bloodstained snow to rest.

All along the banks of the Vistula, from Konigsberg and Dantzig up to Warsaw—that slow river which at the last call shall assuredly give up more dead than any other—the fugitives straggled home-wards. For the Russians paused at their own frontier, and Prussia was still nominally the friend of France. She had still to wear the mask for three long months when she should at last openly side with Russia, only to be beaten again by Napoleon.

Murat was at Königsberg with the Imperial staff, left in supreme command by the Emperor, and already thinking of his own sunny kingdom of the Mediterranean, and the ease and the glory of it. In a few weeks he, too, must tarnish his name.

"I make over the command to you," he said to Prince Eugene; and Napoleon's step-son made an answer which shows, as Eugene showed again and again, that contact with a great man makes for greatness.

"You cannot make it over to me," he replied. "Only the Emperor can do that. You can run away in the night, and the supreme command will devolve on me the next morning."

And what Murat did is no doubt known to the learned reader. Let us at all events pretend that it is, and be true to our generation.

Macdonald, abandoned by Yorck with the Prussian contingent, in great peril, alone in the north, was retreating with the remains of the Tenth Army Corps, wondering whether Königsberg or Dantzig would still be French when he reached them.   On his heels was Wittgenstein, in touch with St. Petersburg and the Emperor Alexander, communicating with Kutusoff at Vilna.   And Macdonald, like the Scotchman and the Frenchman that he was, turned at a critical moment and rent Wittgenstein.   Here was another bulldog in that panic-stricken pack, who turned and snarled and fought while his companions slunk homewards with their tails between their legs.   There were three of such breed—Ney and Macdonald, and Prince Eugene de Beauharnais.

Napoleon was in Paris, getting together in wild haste the new army with which he was yet to frighten Europe into fits.   And Rapp, doggedly fortifying his frozen city, knew that he was to hold Dantzig at any cost—a remote, far-thrown outpost on the Northern sea, cut off from all help, hundreds of miles from the French frontier, nearly a thousand miles from Paris.

At Marienwerder, Barlasch and Désirée found themselves in the midst of that bustle and confusion which attends the arrival or departure of an army corps.   The majority of the men were young and of a dark skin.   They seemed gay, and called out salutations to which Barlasch replied curtly enough.

"They are Italians," said he to his companion; "I know their talk and their manners To you and me, who come from the North, they are like children.   See that one who is dancing. It is some fête. What is to-day?"

"It is New Year's Day," replied Désirée.

"New Year's Day," echoed Barlasch. "Good. And we have been on the road since six o'clock; and I, who have forgotten to wish you——" He paused and called cheerily to the horses, which had covered more than forty miles since leaving their stable at Thorn. "Bon Dieu!" he said in a lower tone, glancing at her beneath the ice-bound rim of his fur cap, "Bon Dieu—what am I to wish you, I wonder?"

Désirée did not answer, but smiled a little and looked straight in front of her.

Barlasch made a movement of the shoulders and eyebrows indicative of a hidden anger.

"We are friends," he asked suddenly, "you and I?"

"Yes."

"We have been friends since—that day—when you were married?"

"Yes," answered Désirée.

"Then between friends," said Barlasch, gruffly; "it is not necessary to smile—like that—when it is tears that are there."

Désirée laughed.

"Would you have me weep?" she asked.

"It would hurt one less," said Barlasch, attending to his horses. They were in the town now, and the narrow streets were crowded. Many sick and wounded were dragging themselves wearily along. A few carts, drawn by starving horses, went slowly down the hill. But there was some semblance of order, and these men had the air and carriage of soldiers under discipline. Barlasch was quick to see it.

"It is the Fourth Corps. The Viceroy's army. They have done well. He is a soldier, who commands them. Ah! There is one I know."

He threw the reins to Désirée, and in a moment he was out on the snow. A man, as old, it would seem, as himself, in uniform and carrying a rifle, was marching past with a few men who seemed to be under his orders, though his uniform was long past recognition. He did not perceive, for some minutes, that Barlasch was coming towards him, and then the process of recognition was slow. Finally, he laid aside his rifle, and the two old men gravely kissed each other.

Quite forgetful of Désirée, they stood talking together for twenty minutes. Then they gravely embraced once more, and Barlasch returned to the sleigh. He took the reins, and urged the horses up the hill without commenting on his encounter, but Désirée could see that he had heard news.

The inn was outside the town, on the road that follows the Vistula northwards to Dirschau and Dantzig. The horses were tired, and stumbled on the powdery snow which was heavy, like sand, and of a sandy colour. Here and there, by the side of the road, were great stains of blood and the remains of a horse that had been killed, and eaten raw. The faces of many of the men were smeared with blood, which had dried on their cheeks and caked there. Nearly all were smoke-grimed and had sore eyes.

At last Barlasch spoke, with the decisive air of one who has finally drawn up a course of action in a difficult position.

"He comes from my own country, that man. You heard us? We spoke together in our patois. I shall not see him again. He has a catarrh. When he coughs there is blood. Alas!"

Désirée glanced at the rugged face half turned away from her. She was not naturally heartless; but she quite forgot to sympathize with the elderly soldier who had caught a cold on the retreat from Moscow; for his friend's grief lacked conviction. Barlasch had heard news which he had decided to keep to himself.

"Has he come from Vilna?" asked Désirée.

"From Vilna—oh yes. They are all from Vilna."

"And he had no news"—persisted she, "of—Captain Darragon?"

"News—oh no! He is a common soldier, and knows nothing of the officers on the staff. We are the same —he and I—poor animals in the ranks. A little gentleman rides up, all sabretasche and gold lace. It is an officer of the staff. 'Go down into the valley and get shot,' he says. And—*bon jour!* we go. No—no. He has no news, my poor comrade."

They were at the inn now, and found the huge yard still packed with sleighs and disabled carriages, and the stables ostentatiously empty.

"Go in," said Barlasch; "and tell them who your father is—say Antoine Sebastian and nothing else. I would do it myself, but when it is so cold as that, the lips are stiff, and I cannot speak German properly. They would find out that I am French, and it is no good being French now. My comrade told me that in Königsberg, Murat himself was ill-received by the burgomaster and such city stuff as that.

It was as Barlasch foretold. For at the name of Antoine Sebastian the innkeeper found horses—in another stable.

It would take a few minutes, he said, to fetch them, and in the meantime there were coffee and some roast meat—his own dinner. Indeed, he could not do enough to testify his respect for Désirée, and his commiseration for her, being forced to travel in such weather through a country infested by starving brigands.

Barlasch consented to come just within the inner door, but refused to sit at the table with Désirée. He took a piece of bread, and ate it standing.

"See you," he said to her when they were left alone, "the good God has made very few mistakes, but there is one thing I would have altered. If He intended us for such a rough life, He should have made the human frame capable of going longer without food. To a poor soldier marching from Moscow to have to stop every three hours and gnaw a piece of horse that has died—and raw—it is not amusing."

He watched Désirée with a grudging eye. For she was young, and had eaten nothing for six freezing hours.

"And for us," he added; "what a waste of time!"

Désirée rose at once with a laugh.

"You want to go," she said. "Come, I am ready."

"Yes," he admitted, "I want to go. I am afraid—name of a dog! I am afraid, I tell you. For I have heard the Cossacks cry, 'Hurrah! Hurrah!' And they are coming."

"Ah!" said Désirée, "that is what your friend told you."

"That, and other things."

He was pulling on his gloves as he spoke, and turned quickly on his heel when the innkeeper entered the room, as if he had expected one of those dread Cossacks of Toula who were half savage. But the innkeeper carried nothing more lethal in his hand than a yellow mug of beer, which he offered to Barlasch. And the old soldier only shook his head.

"There is poison in it," he muttered. "He knows I am a Frenchman."

"Come," said Désirée, with her gay laugh, "I will show you that there is no poison in it."

She took the mug and drank, and handed the measure to Barlasch. It was a poor thin beer, and Barlasch was not one to hide his opinion from the host, to whom he made a reproving grimace when he returned the empty mug. But the effect upon him was nevertheless good, for he took the reins again with a renewed energy, and called to the horses gaily enough.

"Allons," he said; "we shall reach Dantzig safely by nightfall, and there we shall find your husband awaiting us, and laughing at us for our foolish journey."

But being an old man, the beer could not warm his heart for long, and he soon lapsed again into melancholy and silence. Nevertheless, they reached Dantzig by nightfall, and although it was a bitter twilight—colder than the night itself—the streets were full. Men stood in groups and talked. In the brief time required to journey to Thorn something had happened. Something happened every day in Dantzig; for when history wakes from her slumber and moves, it is with a heavy and restless tread.

"What is it?" asked Barlasch of the sentry at the town gate, while they waited for their passports to be returned to them.

"It is a proclamation from the Emperor of Russia—no one knows how it has got here."

"And what does he proclaim—that citizen?"

"He bids the Dantzigers rise and turn us out," answered the soldier, with a grim laugh.

"Is that all?"

"No, comrade, that is not all," was the answer in a graver voice.

"He proclaims that every Pole who submits now will be forgiven and set at liberty; the past, he says, will be committed to an eternal oblivion and a profound silence—those are his words."

"Ah!"

"Yes, and half the defenders of Dantzig are Poles—there are your passports—pass on."

They drove through the dark streets where men like shadows hurried silently about their business.

The Frauengasse seemed to be deserted when they reached it. It was Mathilde who opened the door. She must have been at the darkened window, behind the curtain. Lisa had gone home to her native village in Sammland in obedience to the Governor's orders. Sebastian had not been home all day. Charles had not returned, and there was no news of him.

Barlasch, wiping the snow from his face, watched Désirée, and made no comment.

CHAPTER XXIV.

MATHILDE CHOOSES.

But strong is fate, O Love,
Who makes, who mars, who ends.

DÉSIREÉ was telling Mathilde the brief news of her
futile journey, when a knock at the front door made
them turn from the stairs where they were standing.
It was Sebastian's knock. His hours had been less
regular of late. He came and went without explanation.

When he had freed his throat from his furs, and
laid aside his gloves, he glanced hastily at Désirée,
who had kissed him without speaking.

"And your husband?" he asked curtly.

"It was not he whom we found at Thorn," she
answered. There was something in her father's voice
—in his quick, sidelong glance at her—that caught
her attention. He had changed lately. From a man
of dreams he had been transformed into a man of
action. It is customary to designate a man of action
as a hard man. Custom is the brick wall against

which feeble minds come to a standstill and hinder
the progress of the world. Sebastian had been softened
by action, through which his mental energy had found
an outlet. But to-night he was his old self again—
hard, scornful, incomprehensible.

"I have heard nothing of him," said Désirée.

Sebastian was stamping the snow from his boots.

"But I have," he said, without looking up.

Désirée said nothing. She knew that the secret
she had guarded so carefully—the secret kept by herself and Louis—was hers no longer. In the silence
of the next moments she could hear Barlasch breathing
on his fingers, within the kitchen doorway just behind
her. Mathilde made a little movement. She was on
the stairs, and she moved nearer to the balustrade and
held to it breathlessly. For Charles Darragon's secret
was De Casimir's too.

"These two gentlemen," said Sebastian slowly,
"were in the secret service of Napoleon. They are
hardly likely to return to Dantzig."

"Why not?" asked Mathilde.

"They dare not."

"I think the Emperor will be able to protect his
officers," said Mathilde.

"But not his spies," replied Sebastian coldly.

"Since they wore his uniform, they cannot be
blamed for doing their duty. They are brave enough.

T

They would hardly avoid returning to Dantzig because —because they have outwitted the Tugendbund."

Mathilde's face was colourless with anger, and her quiet eyes flashed. She had been surprised into this sudden advocacy, and an advocate who displays temper is always a dangerous ally. Sebastian glanced at her sharply. She was usually so self-controlled that her flashing eyes and quick breath betrayed her.

"What do you know of the Tugendbund?" he asked.

But she would not answer, merely shrugging her shoulders and closing her thin lips with a snap.

"It is not only in Dantzig," said Sebastian, "that they are unsafe. It is anywhere where the Tugend-bund can reach them."

He turned sharply to Désirée. His wits, cleared by action, told him that her silence meant that she, at all events, had not been surprised. She had, therefore, known already the part played by De Casimir and Charles, in Dantzig, before the war.

"And you," he said, "you have nothing to say for your husband."

"He may have been misled," she said mechanically, in the manner of one making a prepared speech or meeting a foreseen emergency. It had been foreseen by Louis d'Arragon. The speech had been, uncon-sciously, prepared by him.

"You mean, by Colonel de Casimir," suggested

Mathilde, who had recovered her usual quiet. And Désirée did not deny her meaning. Sebastian looked from one to the other. It was the irony of Fate that had married one of his daughters to Charles Darragon, and affianced the other to De Casimir. His own secret, so well kept, had turned in his hand like a concealed weapon.

They were all startled by Barlasch, who spoke from the kitchen door, where he had been standing unobserved or forgotten. He came forward to the light of the lamp hanging overhead.

"That reminds me . . ." he said a second time, and having secured their attention, he instituted a search in the many pockets of his nondescript clothing. He still wore a dirty handkerchief bound over one eye. It served to release him from duty in the trenches or work on the frozen fortifications. By this simple device, coupled with half a dozen bandages in various parts of his person, where a frost-bite or a wound gave excuse, he passed as one of the twenty-five thousand sick and wounded who encumbered Dantzig at this time, and were already dying at the rate of fifty a day.

"A letter . . ." he said, still searching with his maimed hand. "You mentioned the name of the Colonel de Casimir. It was that which recalled to my mind. . . ." He paused, and produced a letter carefully sealed. He turned it over, glancing at the seals with a reproving jerk of the head, which conveyed as clearly as words a shameless confession that he had been frustrated by them . . . "this letter. I was told to give it you, without fail, at the right moment."

It could hardly be the case that he honestly thought this moment might be so described. But he gave the letter to Mathilde with a gesture of grim triumph. Perhaps he was thinking of the cellar in the Palace on the Petrovka at Moscow, and the treasure which he had found there.

"It is from the Colonel de Casimir," he said, "a clever man," he added, turning confidentially to Sebastian, and holding his attention by an upraised hand. "Oh! . . . a clever man."

Mathilde, her face all flushed, tore open the envelope, while Barlasch, breathing on his fingers, watched with twinkling eye and busy lips.

The letter was a long one. Colonel de Casimir was an adept at explanation. There was, no doubt, much to explain. Mathilde read the letter carefully. It was the first she had ever had—a love-letter in its guise—with explanations in it. Love and explanation in the same breath. Assuredly De Casimir was a daring lover.

"He says that Dantzig will be taken by storm,"

she said at length, "and that the Cossacks will spare no one."

"Does it signify," inquired Sebastian in his smoothest voice, " what Colonel de Casimir may say ? "

His grand manner had come back to him. He made a gesture with his hand almost suggestive of a ruffle at the wrist, and clearly insulting to Colonel de Casimir.

"He urges us to quit the city before it is too late," continued Mathilde, in her measured voice, and awaited her father's reply. He took snuff with a cold smile.

"You will not do so ? " she asked. And by way of reply, Sebastian laughed as he dusted the snuff from his coat with his pocket-handkerchief.

"He asks me to go to Cracow with the Grafin, and marry him," said Mathilde finally. And Sebastian only shrugged his shoulders. The suggestion was beneath contempt.

"And . . . ? " he inquired with raised eyebrows.

"I shall do it," replied Mathilde, defiance shining in her eyes.

"At all events," commented Sebastian, who knew Mathilde's mind, and met her coldness with indifference, "you will do it with your eyes open, and not leap in the dark, as Désirée did. I was to blame there; a man is always to blame if he is deceived. With you . . . Bah! you know what the man is. But you do not know, unless he tells you in that letter, that he is even a traitor in his treachery. He has accepted the amnesty offered by the Czar; he has abandoned Napoleon's cause; he has petitioned the Czar to allow him to retire to Cracow, and there live on his estates."

"He has no doubt good reasons for his action," said Mathilde.

"Two carriages full," muttered Barlasch, who had withdrawn to the dark corner near the kitchen door. But no one heeded him.

"You must make your choice," said Sebastian, with the coldness of a judge. "You are of age. Choose."

"I have already chosen," answered Mathilde. "The Gräfin leaves to-morrow. I will go with her."

She had, at all events, the courage of her own opinions—a courage not rare in women, however valueless may be the judgment upon which it is based. And in fairness it must be admitted that women usually have the courage not only of the opinion, but of the consequence, and meet it with a better grace than men can summon in misfortune.

Sebastian dined alone and hastily. Mathilde was locked in her room, and refused to open the door. Désirée cooked her father's dinner while Barlasch made ready to depart on some vague errand in the town.

"There may be news," he said. "Who knows? And afterwards the patron will go out, and it would not be wise for you to remain alone in the house."

"Why not?"

Barlasch turned and looked at her thoughtfully over his shoulder.

"In some of the big houses down in the Niederstadt there are forty and fifty soldiers quartered—diseased, wounded, without discipline. There are others coming. I have told them we have fever in the house. It is the only way. We may keep them out; for the Frauengasse is in the centre of the town, and the soldiers are not needed in this quarter. But you—you cannot lie as I can. You laugh—ah! A woman tells more lies; but a man tells them better. Push the bolts, when I am gone."

After his dinner, Sebastian went out, as Barlasch had predicted. He said nothing to Désirée of Charles or of the future. There was nothing to be said, perhaps. He did not ask why Mathilde was absent. In the stillness of the house, he could probably hear her moving in her rooms upstairs.

He had not been long gone when Mathilde came down, dressed to go out. She came into the kitchen where Désirée was doing the work of the absent Lisa, who had reluctantly gone to her home on the Baltic coast. Mathilde stood by the kitchen table and ate some bread.

"The Gräfin has arranged to quit Dantzig tomorrow," she said. "I am going to ask her to take me with her."

Désirée nodded and made no comment. Mathilde went to the door, but paused there. Without looking round, she stood thinking deeply. They had grown from childhood together—motherless—with a father whom neither understood. Together they had faced the difficulties of life; the hundred petty difficulties attending a woman's life in a strange land, among neighbours who bear the sleepless grudge of unsatisfied curiosity. They had worked together for their daily bread. And now the full stream of life had swept them together from the safe moorings of childhood.

"Will you come too?" asked Mathilde. "All that he says about Dantzig is true."

"No, thank you," answered Désirée, gently enough. "I will wait here. I must wait in Dantzig."

"I cannot," said Mathilde, half excusing herself. "I must go. I cannot help it You understand?"

"Yes," said Désirée, and nothing more.

Had Mathilde asked her the question six months ago, she would have said "No." But she understood now, not that Mathilde could love De Casimir; that was beyond her individual comprehension, but that there was no alternative now.

Soon after Mathilde had gone, Barlasch returned.

"If Mademoiselle Mathilde is going, she will have to go to-morrow," he said. "Those that are coming in at the gates now are the rearguard of the Heudelet Division which was driven out of Elbing by the Cossacks three days ago."

He sat mumbling to himself by the fire, and only turned to the supper which Désirée had placed in readiness for him when she quitted the room and went upstairs. It was he who opened the door for Mathilde, who returned in half an hour. She thanked him absent-mindedly and went upstairs. He could hear the sisters talking together in a low voice in the drawing-room, which he had never seen, at the top of the stairs.

Then Désirée came down, and he helped her to find in a shed in the yard one of those travelling-trunks which he had recognized as being of French manu-facture. He took off his boots, and carried it upstairs for her.

It was ten o'clock before Sebastian came in. He nodded his thanks to Barlasch, and watched him bolt the door. He made no inquiry as to Mathilde, but extinguished the lamp, and went to his room. He never mentioned her name again.

Early the next morning, the girls were astir. But Barlasch was before them, and when Désirée came down, she found the kitchen fire alight. Barlasch was cleaning a knife, and nodded a silent good morning. Désirée's eyes were red, and Barlasch must have noted this sign of grief, for he gave a contemptuous laugh, and continued his occupation.

It was barely daylight when the Gräfin's heavy, old-fashioned carriage drew up in front of the house. Mathilde came down, thickly veiled and in her travelling furs. She did not seem to see Barlasch, and omitted to thank him for carrying her travelling-trunk to the carriage.

He stood on the terrace beside Désirée until the carriage had turned the corner into the Pfaffengasse.

"Bah!" he said, "let her go. There is no stopping them, when they are like that. It is the curse—of the Garden of Eden."

CHAPTER XXV.

A DESPATCH.

In counsel it is good to see dangers; and in execution not to see them unless they be very great.

MATHILDE had told Désirée that Colonel de Casimir made no mention of Charles in his letter to her. Barlasch was able to supply but little further information on the matter.

"It was given to me by the Captain Louis d'Arragon at Thorn," he said. "He handled it as if it were not too clean. And he had nothing to say about it. You know his way, for the rest. He says little, but he knows the look of things. It seemed that he had promised to deliver the letter—for some reason, who knows what? and he kept his promise. The man was not dying by any chance—that De Casimir?"

And his little sharp eyes, reddened by the smoke of camp-fires, inflamed by the glare of sun on snow, searched her face. He was thinking of the treasure.

"Oh no!"

"Was he ill at all?"

"He was in bed," answered Désirée, doubtfully.

Barlasch scratched his head without ceremony, and fell into a long train of thought.

"Do you know what I think?" he said at length. "I think that De Casimir was not ill at all—any more than I am; I, Barlasch. Not so ill, perhaps, as I am, for I have an indigestion. It is always there at the summit of the stomach. It is horse without salt."

He paused and rubbed his chest tenderly.

"Never eat horse without salt," he put in parenthetically.

"I hope never to eat it at all," answered Désirée. "What about Colonel de Casimir?"

He waved her aside as a babbler who broke in upon his thoughts. These seemed to be lodged in his mouth, for, when reflecting, he chewed and mumbled with his lips.

"Listen," he said at length. "This is De Casimir. He goes to bed and lets his beard grow—half an inch of beard will keep any man in the hospital. You nod your head. Yes; I thought so. He knows that the viceroy, with the last of the army, is at Thorn. He keeps quiet. He waits in his roadside inn until the last of the army has gone. He waits until the Russians come, and to them he hands over the Emperor's possessions—all the papers, the maps, the despatches. For that he will be rewarded by the Emperor Alexander, who has already promised pardon to all Poles who have taken arms against Russia and now submit. De Casimir will be allowed to retain his own baggage. He has no loot taken at Moscow—oh no! Only his own baggage. Ah—that man! See, I spit him out."

And it is painful to record that he here resorted to graphic illustration.

"Ah!" he went on triumphantly, "I know. I can see right into the mind of such a man. I will tell you why. It is because I am that sort of man myself."

"You do not seem to have been so successful—since you are poor," said Désirée, with a laugh.

He frowned at her apparently in speechless anger, seeking an answer. But for the moment he could think of none, so he turned to the knives again, which he was cleaning on a board on the kitchen-table. At length he paused and glanced at Désirée.

"And your husband," he said slowly. "Remember that he is a partner with this De Casimir. They hunt together. I know it; for I was in Moscow. Ah! that makes you stand stiffly, and push your chin out."

He went on cleaning the knives, and, without looking at her, seemed to be speaking his own thoughts aloud.

"Yes! He is a traitor. And he is worse than

the other; for he is no Pole, but a Frenchman. And if he returns to France, the Emperor will say: 'Where are my despatches, my maps, my papers, which were given into your care?'"

He finished the thought with three gestures, which seemed to illustrate the placing of a man against a wall and shooting him. His meaning could not be mistaken.

"And that is what the patron means when he says that Monsieur Charles Darragon will not return to Dantzig. I knew that he meant that last night, when he was so angry—on the mat."

"And why did you not tell me?"

Barlasch looked at her thoughtfully for a moment, before replying slowly and impressively.

"Because, if I had told you, you might have decided to quit Dantzig with Mademoiselle Mathilde, and go hunting your husband in a country overrun by desperate fugitives and untamed Cossacks. And I did not want that. I want you here—in Dantzig; in the Frauengasse; in this kitchen; under my hand—so that I can take care of you till the war is over. I—who speak to you—Papa Barlasch, at your service. And there is not another man in the world who will do it so well. No; not one."

And his eyes flashed as he threw the knives into a drawer.

"But why should you do all this for me?" asked

Désirée. "You could have gone home to France—quite easily—and have left us to our fate here in Dantzig. Why did you not go home?"

Barlasch looked at her with surprise, not unmixed with a sudden dumb disappointment. He was preparing to go out according to his wont immediately after breakfast; for Lisa had unconsciously hit the mark when she compared him to a cat. He had the regular and self-contained habits of that unobtrusive friend. He buttoned his rough coat slowly, and looked round the kitchen with eyes dimly wistful. He was very old and ragged and homeless.

"Is it not enough," he said, "that we are friends?"

He went towards the door, but came back and warned her by the familiar upheld finger not to let her attention wander from his words.

"You will be glad yet that I have stayed. It is because I speak a little plainly of your husband that you wish me gone. Bah! What does it matter? All men are alike. We are only men—not angels. And you can go on loving him all the same. You are not particular, you women. You can love anything—even a man like that.

And he went out muttering anathemas on the hearts of all women.

"It seems," he said, "that a woman can love anything."

Which is true; and a very good thing for some of us. For without that Heaven-sent capacity the world could not go on at all.

It was later in the day when Barlasch made his way into the low and smoke-grimed Bier Halle of the Weissen Röss'l. He must have known Sebastian's habits, for he went straight to that corner of the great room where the violin-player usually sat. The stout waitress—a country girl of no intelligence, smiled broadly at the sight of such a ragged customer as she followed him down the length of the sawdust-strewn floor.

Sebastian's face showed no surprise when he looked up and recognized the new-comer. The surrounding tables were empty. It was too early in the evening for the regular customers, whose numbers, moreover, had been sadly thinned during the last few months. For the peaceful Dantzigers, remembering the siege of seven years ago, had mostly fled at the first mention of the word.

Sebastian nodded in answer to Barlasch's somewhat ceremonious bow, and by a gesture invited him to be seated on the chair upon which he had already laid his hand. The atmosphere of the room was warm, and Barlasch laid aside his sheepskin coat, as he had seen the great and the rich divest themselves of their sables. He turned sharply and caught the waitress with an amused smile still on her face. He drew her attention to a little pool of beer on the table, and stood until she had made good this lapse in her duty. Then he pointed to Sebastian's mug of beer and dismissed her giggling, to get one for him of the same size and contents.

Making sure that there was no one within earshot, he waited until Sebastian's dreamy eye met his, and then said—

"It is time we understood each other."

A light of surprise—passing and half-indifferent— flashed into Sebastian's eyes and vanished again at once when he saw Barlasch had meant nothing: made no sign or countersign with his hand.

"By all means, my friend," he answered.

"I delivered your letters," said Barlasch, "at Thorn and at the other places."

"I know; I have already had answers. You would be wise to forget the incident."

Barlasch shrugged his shoulders.

"You were paid," said Sebastian, jumping to a natural conclusion.

"A little," admitted Barlasch, "a small little—but it was not that. I always get paid in advance, when I can. Except by the Emperor. He owes me some— that citizen. It was another question. In the house I am friends with all—with Lisa who has gone— with Mademoiselle Mathilde who has gone — with

U

Mademoiselle Désirée, so-called Madame Darragon, who remains. With all except you. Why should we not be friends?"

"But we are friends——" protested Sebastian, with a bow. As if in confirmation of the statement, he held out his beer-mug, and Barlasch touched it with the rim of his own before drinking. Sebastian's attitude, his bow, his manner of drinking, were those of the Court; Barlasch was distinctly of the camp. But these were strange days, and all society had been turned topsy-turvy by one man.

"Then," said Barlasch, licking his lips, "let us understand one another. You say there will be no siege. I say you are wrong. You think that the Dantzigers will rise in answer to the Emperor Alexander's proclamations, and turn the French out. I say the Dantzigers' stomachs are too big. I say that Rapp will hold Dantzig, and that the Russians will not take it by storm, because they are too weak. There will be a siege, and a long one. Are you and Mademoiselle and I going to sit it out in the Frauengasse together?"

"We shall be honoured to have you as our guest," answered Sebastian, with that levity which went before the Revolution, and was never understood of the people.

Barlasch did not understand it. He glanced doubtfully at his companion, and sipped his beer.

"Then I will begin to-night."

"Begin what, my friend?"

Barlasch waved aside all petty detail.

"My preparations. I go out about ten o'clock—after you are in. I will take the key of the front door, and let myself in when I come back. I shall make two journeys. Under the kitchen floor is a large hollow space. I fill that with bags of corn."

"But where will you get the corn, my friend?"

"I know where to get it—corn and other things. Salt I have already—enough for a year. Other things I can get for three months."

"But we have no money to pay for them."

"Bah!"

"You mean you will steal them," suggested Sebastian, not without a ring of contempt in his mincing voice.

"A soldier never steals," answered Barlasch, carelessly announcing a great truth.

Sebastian laughed. It was obvious that his mind, absorbed in great thought, heeded small things not at all. His companion pushed his fur cap to the back of his head, and ruffled his hair forward.

"That is not all," he said at length. He looked round the vast room, which was almost deserted. The stout waitress was polishing pewter mugs at the bar. "You say you have already had answers to those letters. It is a great organization—your secret society —whatever it is called. It delivers letters all over Prussia—eh? and Poland perhaps—or farther still."

Sebastian shrugged one shoulder, and made no answer for some time.

" I have already told you," he said impatiently, at length, " to forget the incident; you were paid."

By way of reply, the old soldier laboriously emptied his pockets, searching the most remote of them for small copper coins. He counted slowly and carefully until he had made up a thaler.

" But it is not my turn to be paid this time. It is I who pay."

He held out his hand with a pound weight of base metal in it, but Sebastian refused the money with a sudden assumption of his cold and scornful manner, oddly out of keeping with his humble surroundings.

" As between friends——" suggested Barlasch, and, on receiving a more decided negative, returned the coins to his pocket, not without satisfaction.

" I want your friends to pass on a letter for me—I am willing to pay," he said in a whisper. " A letter to Captain Louis d'Arragon—it concerns the happiness of Mademoiselle Désirée. Do not shake your head. Think before you refuse. The letter will be an open one—six words or so—telling the Captain that his cousin, Mademoiselle's husband, is not in Dantzig, and cannot now return here since the last of the rearguard entered the city this morning."

Sebastian seemed to be considering the matter, and Barlasch was quick to combat possible objections.

"The Captain went to Königsberg. He is there now. Your friends can easily find him, and give him the letter. It is of great importance to Mademoiselle. The Captain is not looking for Monsieur Charles Darragon, because he thinks that he is here in Dantzig. Colonel de Casimir assured him that Mademoiselle would find him here. Where is he—that Monsieur Charles—I wonder? It is of great importance to Mademoiselle. The Captain would perhaps continue his search."

"Where is your letter?" asked Sebastian.

By way of reply, Barlasch laid on the table a sheet of paper.

"You must write it," he said. "My hand is injured. I write not badly, you understand. But this evening I do not feel that my hand is well enough."

So, with the sticky, thick ink of the Weissen Röss'l, Sebastian wrote the letter, and Barlasch, forgetting his scholarly acquirements, took the pen and made a mark beneath his own name written at the foot of it.

Then he went out, and left Sebastian to pay for the beer.

CHAPTER XXVI.

ON THE BRIDGE.

They that are above
Have ends in everything

A LAME man was standing on the bridge that crosses the Neuer Pregel from the Kant Strasse—which is the centre of the city of Königsberg—to the island known as the Kneiphof. This bridge is called the Krämer Brücke, and may be described as the heart of the town. From it on either hand diverge the narrow streets that run along the river bank, busy with commerce, crowded with the narrow sleighs that carry wood from the Pregel up into the town.

The wider streets — such as the Kant Strasse, running downhill from the royal castle to the river, and the Kneiphöf'sche Langgasse, leading southward to the Brandenburg gate and the great world—must needs make use of the Krämer Brucke. Here, it may be said, every man in the town must sooner or later pass in the execution of his daily business, whether he go about it on foot or in a sleigh with a pair of horses.

Here the idler and those grave professors from the University, which was still mourning the death of the aged Kant, nearly always passed in their thoughtful and conscientious promenades.

Here this lame man, a cobbler by trade, plying his quiet calling in a house in the Neuer Markt, where the lime-trees grow close to the upper windows, had patiently kept watch for three days. He was, like many lame men, of an abnormal width and weight. He had a large, square, dogged face, which seemed to promise that he would wait there till the crack of doom rather than abandon a quest.

It was very cold—mid-winter within a few miles of the frozen Baltic on the very verge of Russia, at that point where old Europe stretches a long arm out into the unknown. The cobbler was wrapped in a sheepskin coat, which stood out all round him with the stiffness of wood, so that he seemed to be living inside a box. To keep himself warm he occasionally limped across from end to end of the bridge, but never went farther. At times he leant his arms on the stone wall at the Kant Strasse end of the bridge, and looked down into the Lower Fish Market, where women from Pillau and the Baltic shores—mere bundles of clothes—stood over their baskets of fish frozen hard like sticks. It was a silent market. You cannot haggle long when a minute's exposure to the air will give a frost-bite to the end of the nose. The would-be purchaser can scarcely make an effective bargain through a fringe of icicles that rattle against his lips if he open them.

The Pregel had been frozen for three months, with only the one temporary thaw in November which cost Napoleon so many thousands at his broken bridge across the Bérésina. Though no water had flowed beneath this bridge, many strange feet had passed across it.

It had vibrated beneath Napoleon's heavy carriage, under the lumbering guns that Macdonald took northward to blockade Riga. Within the last few weeks it had given passage to the last of the retreating army, a mere handful of heartsick fugitives. Macdonald with his staff had been ignominiously driven across it by the Cossacks who followed hard after them, the great marshal still wild with rage at the defection of Yorck and the Prussian contingent.

And now the Cossacks on their spare and ill-tempered horses passed to and fro, wild men under an untamed leader whose heart was hardened to stone by bereavement. The cobbler looked at them with a countenance of wood. It was hard to say whether he preferred them to the French, or was indifferent to one as to the other. He looked at their boots with professional disdain. For all men must look at the world from their own standpoint and consider mankind in the light of their own interests. Thus those who live

on the greed or the vanity, or batten on the charity of
their neighbour, learn to watch the lips.

The cobbler, by reason of looking at the lower end
of men, attracted little attention from the passer-by.
He who has his eyes on the ground passes unheeded.
For the surest way of awakening interest is to appear
interested. It would seem that this cobbler was waiting for a pair of boots not made in Königsberg. And
on the third day his expressionless black eyes lighted
on feet not shod in Poland, or France, or Germany, nor
yet in square-toed Russia.

The owner of these far-travelled boots was a lightly-
built dark-faced man, with eyes quietly ubiquitous. He
caught the interested glance of the cobbler, and turned
to look at him again with the uneasiness that is bred
of war. The cobbler instantly hobbled towards him.

"Will you help a poor man?" he said.

"Why should I?" was the answer, with one hand
already half out of its thick glove. "You are not
hungry; you have never been starved in your life."

The German was quick enough, but it was not
quite the Prussian German.

The cobbler looked at the speaker slowly.

"An Englishman?" he asked.

And the other nodded.

"Come this way."

The cobbler hobbled towards the Kneiphof, where

the streets are quiet, and the Englishman followed him. At the corner of the Kohl Markt he turned and looked, not at the man, but at his boots.

"You are a sailor?" he said.

"Yes."

"I was told to look for an English sailor—Louis d'Arragon."

"Then you have found me," was the reply.

Still the cobbler hesitated.

"How am I to know it?" he asked suspiciously.

"Can you read?" asked D'Arragon. "I can prove who I am—if I want to. But I am not sure that I want to."

"Oh! it is only a letter—of no importance. Some private business of your own. It comes from Dantzig —written by one whose name begins with 'B.'"

"Barlasch," suggested D'Arragon quietly, as he took from his pocket a paper which he unfolded and held beneath the eyes of the cobbler. It was a passport written in three languages. If the man could read, he was not anxious to boast of an accomplishment so far above his station; but he glanced at the paper, not without a practised skill, to seize the essential parts of it.

"Yes, that is the name," he said, searching in his pockets. "The letter is an open one. Here it is."

In passing the letter, the man made a scarcely

perceptible movement of the hand which might have been a signal.

"No," said D'Arragon, "I do not belong to the Tugendbund or to any other secret society. We have need of no such associations in my country."

The cobbler laughed, not without embarrassment.

"You have a quick eye," he said. "It is a great country, England. I have seen the river full of English ships before Napoleon chased you off the seas."

D'Arragon smiled as he unfolded the letter.

"He has not done it yet," he said, with that spirit which enables mariners of the Anglo-Saxon race to be amused when there is a talk of supremacy on the high seas. He read the letter carefully, and his face hardened.

"I was instructed," said the cobbler, "to give you the letter, and at the same time to inform you that any assistance or facilities you may require will be forthcoming; besides . . ." he broke off and pointed with his thick, leather-stained finger, "that writing is not the writing of him who signs."

"He who signs cannot write at all."

"That writing," went on the cobbler, "is a passport in any German state. He who carries a letter written in that hand can live and travel free anywhere from here to the Rhine or the Danube."

"Then I am lucky in possessing a powerful friend,"

said D'Arragon, "for I know who wrote this letter.
I think I may say he is a friend of mine."

"I am sure of it. I have already been told so,"
said the cobbler. "Have you a lodging in Königsberg?
No. Then you can lodge in my house."

Without awaiting a reply, which he seemed to
consider a foregone conclusion, he limped down the
Kohl Markt towards the steps leading to the river,
which in winter is a thoroughfare.

"I live in the Neuer Markt," he said breathlessly,
as he laboured onwards. "I have waited for you three
days on that bridge. Where have you been all this time?"

"Avoiding the French," replied D'Arragon curtly.
Respecting his own affairs he was reticent, as com-
manders and other lonely men must always be. They
walked side by side on the dusty and trodden ice
without further speech. At the steps from the river
to Neuer Markt, D'Arragon gave the lame man his
hand, and glanced a second time at the fingers which
clasped his own. They had not been born to toil, but
had had it thrust upon them.

They crossed the Neuer Markt together, and went
into that house where the linden grows so close as to
obscure the windows. And the lodging offered to
Louis was the room in which Charles Darragon had
slept in his wet clothes six months earlier. So small
is the world in which we live, and so narrow are the

circles drawn by Fate around human existence and endeavour.

The cobbler having shown his visitor the room, and pointed out its advantages, was turning to go when D'Arragon, who was laying aside his fur coat, seemed to catch his attention, and he paused on the threshold.

"There is French blood in your veins," he said abruptly.

"Yes—a little."

"So. I thought there must be. You reminded me—it was odd, the way you laid aside your coat— reminded me of a Frenchman who lodged here for one night. He was like you, too, in build and face. He was a spy, if you please—one of the French Emperor's secret police. I was new at the work then, but still I suspected there was something wrong about him. I took his boots—a pretext of mending them. I locked him in. He got out of that window, if you please, without his boots. He followed me, and learnt much that he was not meant to know. I have since heard it from others. He did the Emperor a great service—that man. He saved his life, I think, from assassination in Dantzig. And he did me an ill turn—but it was my own carelessness. I thought to make a thaler by lodging him, and he was tricking me all the while."

"What was his name?" asked D'Arragon.

"Oh—I forgot the name he gave. It was a false

one. He was disguised as a common soldier—and he was in reality an officer of the staff. But I know the name of the officer to whom he wrote his report of his night's lodging here—his colleague in the secret police, it would seem."

"Ah!" said D'Arragon, busying himself with his haversack.

"It was De Casimir—a Polish name. And in the last two days I have heard of him. He has accepted the Emperor's amnesty. He has married a beautiful woman, and is living like a prince at Cracow. All this since the siege of Dantzig began. In time of war there is no moment to lose, eh?"

"And the other? He who slept in this room. Has he passed through Königsberg again."

"No, that he has not. If he had, I should have seen him. You can believe me, I wanted to see him I was at my place on the bridge all the time—while the French occupied Königsberg—when the last of them hurried away a month ago with the Cossacks close behind. No. I should have seen him, and known him. He is not on this side of the Niemen, that fine young gentleman. Now, what can I do to help you to-morrow?"

"You can help me on the way to Vilna," answered D'Arragon.

"You will never get there."

"I will try," said the sailor.

CHAPTER XXVII.

A FLASH OF MEMORY.

Nothing can cover his high fame but Heaven :
No pyramids set off his memories,
But the eternal substance of his greatness
To which I leave him.

"WHY I will not let you go out into the streets," said Barlasch one February morning, stamping the snow from his boots. "Why I will not let you go out into the streets?"

He turned and followed Désirée towards the kitchen, after having carefully bolted the heavy oaken door which had been strengthened as if to resist a siege. Désirée's face had that clear pallor which marks an indoor life; but Barlasch, weather-beaten, scorched and wrinkled, showed no sign of having endured a month's siege in an overcrowded city.

"I will tell you why I will not let you go into the streets. Because they are not fit for any woman to go into—because if you walked from here to the Rathhaus you would see sights that would come back to you in your sleep, and wake you from it, when you are an old woman. Do you know what they do with their dead? They throw them outside their doors—with nothing to cover their starved nakedness—as Lisa put her ashes in the street every morning. And the cart goes round, as the dustman's cart used to go in times of peace, and, like the dustman's cart, it drops part of its load, and the dust that blows round it is the infection of typhus. That is why you cannot go into the streets."

He unbuttoned his fur coat and displayed a smart new uniform; for Rapp had put his miserable army into new clothes, with which many of the Dantzig warehouses had been filled by Napoleon's order at the beginning of the war.

"There," he said, laying a small parcel on the table, "there is my daily ration. Two ounces of horse, one ounce of salt beef, the same as yesterday. One does not know how long we shall be treated so generously. Let us keep the beef—we may come to want some day."

And giving a hoarse laugh, he lifted a board in the floor, beneath which he hoarded his stores.

"Will you cook your *déjeuner* yourself," asked Désirée. "I have something else for my father."

"And what have you?" asked Barlasch curtly, "you are not keeping anything hidden from me?"

"No," answered Désirée, with a laugh at the sternness of his face, "I will give him a piece of the ham which was left over from last night."

"Left over?" echoed Barlasch, going close to her and looking up into her face, for she was two inches taller than he. "Left over? Then you did not eat your supper last night?"

"Neither did you eat yours, for it is there under the floor."

Barlasch turned away with a gesture of despair. He sat down in the high armchair that stood on the hearth, and tapped on the floor with one foot in pessimistic thought.

"Ah! the women, the women," he muttered, looking into the smouldering fire. "Lies—all lies. You said that your supper was very nice," he shouted at her over his shoulder.

"So it was," answered she gaily, "so it is still."

Barlasch did not rise to her lighter humour. He sat in reflection for some minutes. Then his thoughts took their usual form of a muttered aside.

"It is a case of compromise. Always like that. The good God had to compromise with the first woman he created almost at once. And men have done it ever since—and have never had the best of it. See here," he said aloud, turning to Désirée, "I will make a bargain with you. I will eat my last night's supper, here at this table, now, if you will eat yours."

X

" Agreed."

" Are you hungry ? " asked Barlasch, when the scanty meal was set out before him.

" Yes."

" So am I."

He laughed quite gaily now, and the meal was not without a certain air of festivity, though it consisted of nothing better than two ounces of horse and half an ounce of ham eaten in company of that rye-bread made with one-third part of straw which Rapp allowed the citizens to buy.

For Rapp had first tamed his army, and was now taming the Dantzigers. He had effected discipline in his own camp by getting his regiments into shape, by establishing hospitals (which were immediately filled), and by protecting the citizens from the depredations of the starving fugitives who had been poured pell-mell into the town.

Then he turned his attention to the Dantzigers, who were openly or secretly opposed to him. He seized their churches and turned them into stores; their schools he used for hospitals, their monasteries for barracks. He broke into their cellars, and took the wine for the sick. Their storehouses he placed under the strictest guard, and no man could claim possession of his own goods.

" We are," he said in effect, with that grim Alsatian

humour which the Prussians were slow to understand ; "we are one united family in a narrow house, and it is I who keep the storeroom key."

Barlasch had proved to be no false prophet. His secret store escaped the vigilance of the picket, whom he himself conducted to the cellars in the Frauengasse. Although he was sparing enough, he could always provide Désirée with anything for which she expressed a wish, and even forestalled those which she left unspoken. In return he looked for absolute obedience, and after their frugal breakfast he took her to task for depriving herself of such food as they could afford.

"See you," he said, "a siege is a question of the stomach. It is not the Russians we have to fight; for they will not fight. They sit outside and wait for us to die of cold, of starvation, of typhus. And we are obliging them at the rate of two hundred a day. Yes, each day Rapp is relieved of the responsibility of two hundred mouths that drop open and require nothing more. Be greedy—eat all you have, and hope for release to-morrow, and you die. Be sparing—starve yourself from parsimony or for the love of some one who will eat your share and forget to thank you, and you will die of typhus. Be careful, and patient, and selfish—eat a little, take what exercise you can, cook your food carefully with salt, and you will live. I was in a siege thirty years before you were born, and I am alive yet, after many others. Obey me and we will get through the siege of Dantzig, which is only just beginning."

Then suddenly he gave way to anger, and banged his hand down on the table.

"But, sacred name of thunder, do not make me believe you have eaten when you have not," he shouted. "Never do that."

Carried away by the importance of this question, he said many things which cannot be set before the eyes of a generation sensitive to plainness of speech, and only tolerant of it in suggestions of impropriety.

"And the patron," he ended abruptly, "how is he?"

"He is not very well," answered Désirée. Which answer did not satisfy Barlasch, who insisted on taking off his boots, and going upstairs to see Sebastian.

It was a mere nothing, the invalid said. Such food did not suit him.

"You have been accustomed to live well all your life," answered Barlasch, looking at him with the puzzled light of a baffled memory in his eye which always came when he looked at Désirée's father. "One must see what can be done."

And he went out forthwith to return after an hour and more with a chicken freshly killed. Désirée did not ask him where he had procured it. She had given

up such inquiries, for Barlasch always confessed quite
bluntly to theft, and she did not know whether to
believe him or not.

But the change of diet had no beneficial effect, and
the next day Désirée sent Barlasch to the house of
the doctor whose practice lay in the Frauengasse. He
came and shook his head bluntly. For even an old
doctor may be hardened at the end of his life by
an orgy, as it were, of death.

"I could cure him," he said, "if there were no
Russians outside the walls; if I could give him fresh
milk and good brandy and strong soup."

But even Barlasch could not find milk in Dantzig.
The brandy was forthcoming, and the fresh meat; the
soup Désirée made with her own hands. Sebastian
had not been the same man since the closing of the
roads and the gradual death of his hopes that the
Dantzigers would rise against the soldiers that thronged
their streets. At one time it would have been easy
to carry out such a movement, and to throw themselves
and their city upon the mercy of the Russians. But
Dantzig awoke to this possibility too late, when Rapp's
iron hand had closed in upon it. He knew his own
strength so well that he treated with a contemptuous
leniency such citizens as were convicted of communicating with the enemy.

Sebastian's friends seemed to have deserted him.

Perhaps it was not discreet to be seen in the company of one who had come under Napoleon's displeasure. Some had quitted the city after hurriedly concealing their valuables in their gardens, behind the chimneys, beneath the floors, where it is to be supposed they still lie hidden. Others were among the weekly thousand or twelve hundred who were carted out by the Oliva Gate to be thrown into huge trenches, while the waiting Russians watched from their lines on the heights of Langfuhr.

It was true that news continued to filter in, and never quite ceased, all through the terrible twelve months that were to follow. More especially did news that was unfavourable to the French find its way into the beleaguered city. But it was not authentic news, and Sebastian gathered little comfort from the fact—not unknown to the whispering citizens—that Rapp himself had heard nothing from the outer world since the Elbing mail-cart had been turned back by the first of the Cossacks on the night of the seventh of January.

Perhaps Sebastian had that most fatal of maladies—to which nearly all men come at last—weariness of life.

"Why don't you fortify yourself, and laugh at fortune?" asked Barlasch, twenty years his senior, as he stood sturdily on his stocking-feet at the sick man's bedside.

"I take what my daughter gives me," protested Sebastian, half peevishly.

"But that does not suffice," answered the materialist. "It does not suffice to swallow evil fortune—one must digest it."

Sebastian made no answer. He was a quiet patient, and lay all day with wide-open, dreaming eyes. He seemed to be waiting for something. This, indeed, was his mental attitude as presented to his neighbours, and perhaps to the few friends he possessed in Dantzig. He had waited through the years during which Désirée had grown to womanhood. He waited on doggedly through the first month of the siege, without enthusiasm, without comment—without hope, perhaps. He seemed to be waiting now to get better.

"He has made little or no progress," said the doctor, who could only give a passing glance at his patients, for he was working day and night. He had not time to beat about the bush, as his kind heart would have liked, for he had known Désirée all her life.

It was Shrove Tuesday, and the streets were full of revellers. The Neapolitans and other Southerners had made great preparations for the carnival, and the Governor had not denied them their annual licence. They had built a high car in one of the entrance yards to the Marienkirche; and finding that the ancient arch would not allow the erection to pass out into the street, they had pulled down the pious handiwork of a bygone generation.

The shouts of these merrymakers could be dimly heard through the double windows, but Sebastian made no inquiry as to the meaning of the cry. A sort of lassitude—the result of confinement within doors, of insufficient food, of waning hope—had come over Désirée. She listened heedlessly to the sounds in the streets through which the dead were passing to the Oliva Gate, while the living danced by in their hideous travesty of rejoicing.

It was dusk when Barlasch came in.

"The streets," he said, "are full of fools, dressed as such." Receiving no answer, he crossed the room to where Désirée sat, treading noiselessly, and stood in front of her, trying to see her averted face. He stooped down and peered at her until she could no longer hide her tear-stained eyes.

He made a wry face and a little clicking noise with his tongue, such as the women of his race make when they drop and break some household utensil. Then he went back towards the bed. Hitherto he had always observed a certain ceremoniousness of manner in the sick chamber. He laid this aside this evening, and sat down on a chair that stood near.

Thus they remained in a silence which seemed to increase with the darkness. At length the stillness became so marked that Barlasch slowly turned his head towards the bed. The same instinct had come to Désirée at the same moment.

They both rose and groped their way towards Sebastian. Désirée found the flint and struck it. The sulphur burnt blue for interminable moments, and then flared to meet the wick of the candle. Barlasch watched Désirée as she held the light down to her father's face. Sebastian's waiting was over. Barlasch had not needed a candle to recognize death.

From Désirée his bright and restless eyes turned slowly towards the dead man's face—and he stepped back.

"Ah!" he said, with a hoarse cry of surprise, "now I remember. I was always sure that I had seen his face before. And when I saw it it was like that—like the face of a dead man. It was on the Place de la Nation, on a tumbrel—going to the guillotine. He must have escaped, as many did, by some accident or mistake."

He went slowly to the window, holding his shaggy head between his two clenched hands as if to spur his memory to an effort. Then he turned and pointed to the silent form on the bed.

"That is a noble of France," he said; "one of the greatest. And all France thinks him dead this twenty years. And I cannot remember his name—goodness of God—I cannot remember his name!"

CHAPTER XXVIII.

VILNA.

It is our trust
That there is yet another world to mend
All error and mischance

LOUIS D'ARRAGON knew the road well enough from Königsberg to the Niemen. It runs across a plain, flat as a table, through which many small streams seek their rivers in winding beds. This country was not thinly inhabited, though the villages had been stripped, as foliage is stripped by a cloud of locusts. Each cottage had its ring of silver birch-trees to protect it from the winds which sweep from the Baltic and the steppe. These had been torn and broken down by the retreating army, in a vain hope of making fire with green wood.

It was quite easy to keep in the steps of the retreating army, for the road was marked by recumbent forms huddled on either side. Few vehicles had come so far, for the broken country near to Vilna and around Kowno had presented slopes up which the starving horses were unable to drag their load.

D'Arragon reached Kowno without mishap, and

there found a Russian colonel of Cossacks who proved friendly enough, and not only appreciated the value of his passport and such letters of recommendation as he had been able to procure at Königsberg, but gave him others, and forwarded him on his journey.

He still nourished a lingering belief in De Casimir's word. Charles must have been left behind at Vilna to recover from his exhaustion. He would, undoubtedly, make his way westward as soon as possible. He might have got away to the South. Any one of these huddled human landmarks might be Charles Darragon.

Louis was essentially a thorough man. The sea is a mistress demanding a whole and concentrated attention—and concentration soon becomes a habit. Louis did not travel at night, for fear of passing Charles on the road, alive or dead. He knew his cousin better than any in the Frauengasse had learnt to know this gay and inconsequent Frenchman. A certain cunning lay behind the happy laugh—a great capacity was hidden by the careless manner. If ready wit could bring man through the dangers of the retreat, Charles had as good a chance of surviving as any.

Nevertheless, Louis rarely passed a dead man on the road, but drew up, and quitting his sleigh, turned over the body, which was almost invariably huddled with its back offered to the deadly, prevailing North wind. Against each this wind had piled a sloping bank of that fine snow which, even in the lightest breeze, drifts over the surface of the land like an ivory mist, waist high, and cakes the clothes. In a high wind it will rise twenty feet in the air, and blind any who try to face it.

As often as not a mere glance sufficed to show that this was not Charles, for few of the bodies were clad. Many had been stripped, while still living, by their half-frozen comrades. But sometimes Louis had to dust the snow from strange bearded faces before he could pass on with a quick sigh of relief.

Beyond Kowno, the country is thinly populated, and spreading pine-forests bound the horizon. The Cossacks—the wild men of Toula, who reaped the laurels of the rearguard fighting—were all along the road. D'Arragon frequently came upon a picket—as often as not the men were placidly sitting on a frozen corpse, as on a seat—and stopped to say a few words and gather news.

"You will find your friend at Vilna," said one young officer, who had been attached to General Wilson's staff, and had many stories to tell of the energetic and indefatigable English commissioner. "At Vilna we took twenty thousand prisoners—poor devils who came and asked us for food—and I don't know how many officers. And if you see Wilson there, remember me to him. If Napoleon has need to hate one man more than another for this business, it is that firebrand, Wilson. Yes, you will assuredly find your cousin at Vilna among the prisoners. But you must not linger by the road, for they are being sent back to Moscow to rebuild that which they have caused to be destroyed."

He laughed and waved his gloved hand as D'Arragon drove on.

After the broken land and low abrupt hills of Kowno, the country was flat again until the valley of the Vilia opened out. And here, almost within sight of Vilna, D'Arragon drove down a short hill which must ever be historic. He drove slowly, for on either side were gun-carriages deep sunken in the snow where the French had left them. This hill marked the final degeneration of the Emperor's army into a shapeless rabble hopelessly flying before an exhausted enemy.

Half on the road and half in the ditch were hundreds of carriages which had been hurriedly smashed up to provide firewood. Carts, still laden with the booty of Moscow, stood among the trees. Some of them contained small square boxes of silver coin, brought by Napoleon to pay his army and here abandoned. Silver coin was too heavy to carry. The rate of exchange had long been sixty francs in silver for a gold napoleon or a louis. The cloth coverings of the cushions had been torn off to shape into rough garments; the straw stuffing had been eaten by the horses.

Inside the carriages were—crouching on the floor—the frozen bodies of fugitives too badly wounded or too ill to attempt to walk. They had sat there till death came to them. Many were women. In one carriage four women, in silks and fine linen, were huddled together. Their furs had been dragged from them either before or after death.

Louis stopped at the bottom and looked back. De Casimir at all events had succeeded in surmounting this obstacle which had proved fatal to so many—the grave of so many hopes—God's rubbish-heap, where gold and precious stones, silks and priceless furs, all that greedy men had schemed and striven and fought to get, fell from their hands at last.

Vilna lies all down a slope—a city built upon several hills—and the Vilia runs at the bottom. That Way of Sorrow, the Smolensk Road, runs eastward by the river bank, and here the rearguard held the Cossacks in check while Murat hastily decamped, after dark, westwards to Kowno. The King of Naples, to whom Napoleon gave the command of his broken army quite gaily—"à vous, Roi de Naples," he is reported to have said, as he hurried to his carriage—Murat abandoned his sick and wounded; did not even warn the stragglers.

D'Arragon entered the city by the narrow gate known as the Town Gate, through which, as through that greater portal of Moscow, every man must pass bareheaded.

"The Emperor is here," were the first words spoken to him by the officer on guard.

But the streets were quiet enough, and the winner in this great game of chance maintained the same unostentatious silence in victory as that which, in the hour of humiliation, had baffled Napoleon.

It was almost night, and D'Arragon had been travelling since daylight. He found a lodging, and, having secured the comfort of the horse provided by the lame shoemaker of Königsberg, he went out into the streets in search of information.

Few cities are, to this day, so behind the times as Vilna. The streets are still narrow, winding, ill-paved, ill-lighted. When D'Arragon quitted his lodging, he found no lights at all, for the starving soldiers had climbed to the lamps for the sake of the oil, which they had greedily drunk. It was a full moon, however, and the patrols at the street corners were willing to give such information as they could. They were strangers to Vilna like Louis himself, and not without suspicion; for this was a city which had bidden the French welcome. There had been dancing and revelry on the outward march. The citizens themselves were afraid of the strange, wild-eyed men who returned to them from Moscow.

At last, in the Episcopal Palace, where head-quarters had been hurriedly established, Louis found the man he sought, the officer in charge of the arrangements for despatching prisoners into Russia and to Siberia. He was a grizzled warrior of the old school, speaking only French and Russian. He was tired out and hungry, but he listened to Louis' story.

"There is the list," he said, "it is more or less complete. Many have called themselves officers who never held a commission from the Emperor Napoleon. But we have done what we can to sort them out.'

So Louis sat down in the dimly lighted room and deciphered the names of those officers who had been left behind, detained by illness or wounds or the lack of spirit to persevere.

"You understand," said the Russian, returning to his work, "I cannot afford the time to help you. We have twenty-five thousand prisoners to feed and keep alive."

"Yes—I understand," answered Louis, who had the seaman's way of making himself a part of his surroundings.

The old colonel glanced at him across the table with a grim smile.

"The Emperor," he said, "was sitting in that chair an hour ago. He may come back at any moment."

"Ah!" said Louis, following the written lines with a pencil.

But no interruption came, and at last the list was finished. Charles was not among the officers taken prisoner at Vilna.

"Well?" inquired the Russian, without looking up.

"Not there."

The old officer took a sheet of paper and hurriedly wrote a few words on it.

"Try the Basile Hospital to-morrow morning," he said. "That will gain you admittance. It is to be cleared out by the Emperor's orders. We have about twenty thousand dead to dispose of as well—but they are in no hurry."

He laughed grimly, and bade Louis good night.

"Come to me again," he called out after him, drawn by a sudden chord of sympathy to this stranger, who had the rare capacity of confining himself to the business in hand.

By daybreak the next morning Louis was at the hospital of St. Basile. It had been prepared by the Duc de Bassano under Napoleon's orders when Vilna was selected as the base of the great army. When the Russians entered Vilna after the retreating remnant of Murat's rabble, they found the dead and the dying in the streets and the market-place. Some had made fires and had lain themselves down around them—to die. Others were without food or firing, almost without clothes. Many were barefoot. All, officers and men alike, were in rags. It was a piteous sight; for half of these men were no longer human. Some were gnawing at their own limbs. Many were blind, others had lost their speech or hearing. Nearly all were marred by some disfigurement—some terrible sore, the result of a frozen wound, of frostbite, of scurvy, of gangrene.

The Cossacks, half civilized as they were, wild with the excitement of killing and the chase of a human quarry, stood aghast in the streets of Vilna.

When the Emperor arrived, he set to work to clear the streets first, to get these piteous men indoors. There was no question yet of succouring them. It was not even possible to feed them all. The only thought was to find them some protection against the ruthless cold.

The first thought was, of course, directed to the hospitals. They looked in and saw a storehouse of the dead. The dead could wait; but the living must be housed.

So the dead waited, and it was their turn now at the St. Basile Hospital, where Louis presented himself at dawn.

"Looking for some one?" asked a man in uniform, who must have been inside the hospital, for he hurried down the steps with a set mouth and quailing eyes.

"Yes."

"Then don't go in—wait here."

Louis looked in and took the doctor's advice. The

dead were stored in the passages, one on the top of the other, like bales of goods in a warehouse.

Some attempt seemed to have been made to clear the wards, but those whose task it had been had not had time to do more than drag the dead out into the passage.

The soldiers were now at work in the lower passage. Carts began to arrive. An officer told off to this dread duty came up hurriedly smoking a cigarette, his high fur collar about his ears. He glanced at Louis, and bowed to him.

" Looking for some one ? " he asked.

" Yes."

" Then stand here beside me. It is I who have to keep count. They say there are eight thousand in here. They will be carried past here to the carts. Have a cigarette."

It is hard to talk when the thermometer registers more than twenty degrees of frost, for the lips stiffen and contract into wrinkles like the lips of a very old woman. Perhaps neither of the watchers was in the humour to begin an acquaintance.

They stood side by side, stamping their feet to keep the blood going, without speaking. Once or twice Louis stepped forward, and at a signal from the officer the bearers stopped. But Louis shook his head, and they passed on. At midday the officer was relieved, his place being taken by another, who bowed stiffly to Louis and took no more notice of him. For war either hardens or softens. It never leaves a man as it found him.

All day the work was carried on. Through the hours this procession of the bearded dead went silently by. At the invitation of a sergeant, Louis took some soup and bread from the soldiers' table. The men laughingly apologized for the quality of both.

Towards evening the officer who had first come on duty returned to his work.

"Not yet?" he asked, offering the inevitable cigarette.

"Not yet," answered Louis, and even as he spoke he stepped forward and stopped the bearers. He brushed aside the matted hair and beard.

" Is that your friend?" asked the officer.

"Yes."

It was Charles at last.

"The doctor says these have been dead two months," volunteered the first bearer, over his shoulder.

"I am glad you have found him," said the officer, signing to the men to go on with their burden. "It is better to know—is it not?"

"Yes," answered Louis slowly. "It is better to know."

And something in his voice made the Russian officer turn and watch him as he went away.

CHAPTER XXIX.

THE BARGAIN.

Like plants in mines which never saw the sun,
But dream of him and guess where he may be,
And do their best to climb and get to him.

"OH yes," Barlasch was saying, "it is easier to die—
it is that that you are thinking—it is easier to die."

Désirée did not answer. She was sitting in the
little kitchen at the back of the house in the Frauengasse. For they had no firing now, and were burning
the furniture. Her father had been buried a week.
The siege was drawn closer than ever. There was
nothing to eat, nothing to do, no one to talk to. For
Sebastian's political friends did not dare to come
near his house. Désirée was alone in this hopeless
world with Barlasch, who was on duty now in one
of the trenches near the river. He went out in the
morning, and only returned at night. He had just
come in, and she could see by the light of the single
candle that his face was grey and haggard, with deep
lines drawn downwards from eyes to chin. Désirée's

own face had lost all its roundness and the bloom of her northern girlhood.

Barlasch glanced at her, and bit his lip. He had brought nothing with him. At one time he had always managed to bring something to the house every day—a chicken, or a turnip, or a few carrots. But to-night there was nothing. And he was tired out. He did not sit down, however, but stood breathing on his fingers and rubbing them together to restore circulation. He pushed the candle farther forward on the table, so that it cast a better light upon her face.

"Yes," he said, "it is often so. I, who speak to you, have seen it so a dozen times in my life. When it is easier to sit down and die. Bah! That is a fine thing to do—a brave thing—to sit down and die."

"I am not going to do it, so do not make that mistake," said Désirée, with a laugh that had no mirth in it.

"But you would like to. Listen. It is not what you feel that matters; it is what you do. Remember that."

There was an unusual vigour in his voice. Of late, since the death of Sebastian, Barlasch seemed to have fallen victim to the settled apathy which lives within a prison wall and broods over a besieged city. It is a sort of silent mourning worn by the soul for a lost liberty. Dantzig had soon succumbed to it, for the citizens had not even the satisfaction of being quite sure that they were deserving of the world's sympathy. It soon spread to the soldiers who were defending a Prussian city for a French Emperor who seemed to have forgotten them.

But to-night Barlasch seemed to be more energetic. Désirée looked round over her shoulder. He had not laid on the table any contribution to a bare larder; and yet his manner was that of one who has prepared a surprise and is waiting to enjoy its effect. He was restless, moving from one foot to another, rubbing together his crooked fingers and darting sidelong glances at her face.

"What is it?" she asked suddenly, and Barlasch gave a start as if he had been detected in some deceit. He bustled forward to the smouldering fire and held his hands over it.

"It is that it is very cold to-night," he answered, with that exaggerated ease of manner with which the young and the simple seek to conceal embarrassment. "Tell me, mademoiselle, what have we for supper to-night? It is I who will cook it. To-night we will keep a *fête*. There is that piece of beef for you. I know a way to make it appetizing. For me there is my portion of horse. It is the friend of man—the horse."

He laughed and made an effort to be gay, which had a poignant pathos in it that made Désirée bite her lip.

"What *fête* is it that we are to keep?" she asked, with a wan smile. Her kind blue eyes had that glitter in them which is caused by a constant and continuous hunger. Six months ago they had only been gay and kind, now they saw the world as it is, as it always must be so long as the human heart is capable of happiness and the human reason recognizes the rarity of its attainment.

"The *fête* of St. Matthias—my *fête*, mademoiselle."

"But I thought your name was Jean."

"So it is. But I keep my *fête* at St. Matthias, because on that day we won a battle in Egypt. We will have wine—a bottle of wine—eh?"

So Barlasch prepared a great feast which was to be celebrated by Désirée in the dining-room, where he lighted a fire, and by himself in the kitchen. For he held strongly to a code of social laws which the great Revolution had not succeeded in breaking. And one of these laws was that it would be in some way degrading to Désirée to see him eat.

He was a skilled and delicate cook, only hampered by that insatiable passion for economy which is the dominant characteristic of the peasant of Northern France. To-night, however, he was reckless, and Désirée could hear him searching in his secret hiding-place beneath the floor for concealed condiments and herbs.

"There," he said, when he set the dish before her, "eat it with an easy mind. There is nothing unclean in it. It is not rat or cat or the liver of a starved horse, such as we others eat and ask no better. It is all clean meat."

He poured out wine, and stood in the darkened doorway watching her drink it. Then he went away to his own meal in the kitchen, leaving Désirée vaguely uneasy—for he was not himself to-night. She could hear him muttering as he ate and moved hither and thither in the kitchen. At short intervals he came and looked in at the door to make sure that she was doing full honour to St. Matthias. When she had finished, he came into the room.

"Ah!" he said, glancing at her suspiciously and rubbing his hands together. "That strengthens, eh?—that strengthens. We others who lead a rough life—we know that a little food and a glass of wine fit one out for any enterprise, for—well, any catastrophe."

And Désirée knew in a flash of comprehension that the food and the wine and the forced gaiety were nothing but preliminaries to bad news.

"What is it?" she asked a second time. "Is it . . . bombardment?"

"Bombardment," he laughed, "they cannot shoot, those Cossacks. It is only the French who understand artillery."

"Then what is it ?—for you have something to tell me, I know."

He ruffled his shock-head of white hair, with a grimace of despair.

"Yes," he admitted, " it is news."

"From outside ?" cried Désirée, with a sudden break in her voice.

"From Vilna," answered Barlasch. He came into the room, and went past her towards the fire, where he put the logs together carefully.

"It is that he is alive," said Désirée, " my husband."

" No, it is not that," Barlasch corrected. He stood with his back to her, vaguely warming his hands. He had no learning, nor manners, nor any polish · nothing but those instincts of the heart that teach the head. And his instinct bade him turn his back on Désirée, and wait in silence until she had understood his meaning.

" Dead ? " she asked, in a whisper.

And, still warming his hands, he nodded his head vigorously. He waited a long time for her to speak, and at last broke the silence himself without looking round.

"Troubles," he said, " troubles for us all. There is no avoiding them. One can only push against them as against your cold wind of Dantzig that comes from the sea. One can only push on. You must push, mademoiselle."

"When did he die?" asked Désirée; "where?"

"At Vilna, three months ago. He has been dead three months. I knew he was dead when you came back to the inn at Thorn, and told me that you had seen De Casimir. De Casimir had left him dying— that liar. You remember, I met a comrade on the road —one of my own country—he told me that they had left ten thousand dead at Vilna, and twenty thousand prisoners little better than dead. And I knew then that De Casimir had left him there dying, or dead."

He glanced back at her over his shoulder, and at the sight of her face made that little click in his throat which, in peasant circles, denotes a catastrophe. Then he shook his head slowly from side to side.

"Listen," he said roughly, "the good God knows best. I knew when I saw you first, that day in June, in this kitchen, that you were beginning your troubles; for I knew the reputation of Monsieur, your husband. He was not what you thought him. A man is never what a woman thinks him. But he was worse than most. And this trouble that has come to you is chosen by the good God—and he has chosen the least in his sack for you. You will know it some day—as I know it now."

"You know a great deal," said Désirée, who was

quick in speech, and he swung round on his heel to meet her spirit.

"You are right," he said, pointing his accusatory finger. "I know a great deal about you—and I am a very old man."

"How did you learn this news from Vilna?" she asked, and his hand went up to his mouth as if to hide his thoughts and control his lips.

"From one who comes straight from there—who buried your husband there."

Désirée rose and stood with her hands resting on the table, looking at the persistent back again turned towards her.

"Who?" she asked, in little more than a whisper.

"The Captain—Louis d'Arragon."

"And you have spoken to him to-day—here, in Dantzig?"

Barlasch nodded his head.

"Was he well?" asked Désirée, with a spontaneous anxiety that made Barlasch turn slowly and look at her from beneath his great brows.

"Oh, he was well enough," he answered, "he is made of steel, that gentleman. He was well enough, and he has the courage of the devil. There are some fishermen who come from Zoppot to sell their fish. They steal through the Russian lines—on the ice of the river at night and come to our outposts at daylight.

One of them said my name this morning. I looked at him. He was wrapped up only to show the eyes. He drew his scarf aside. It was the Captain d'Arragon."

"And he was well?" asked Désirée again, as if nothing else in the world mattered.

"Oh, mon Dieu, yes," cried Barlasch, impatiently, "he was well, I tell you. Do you know why he came?"

Désirée had sat down at the table again, where she leant her arms and rested her chin in the palms of her two hands; for she was weakened by starvation, and confinement, and sorrow.

"No," she answered.

"He came because he had learnt that the patron was dead. It was known in Konigsberg a week ago. It is known all over Germany; that quiet old gentleman who scraped a fiddle here in the Frauengasse. And it is only I, in all the world, who know that he was a greater man in Paris than ever he was in Germany—with his Tugendbund—and I cannot remember his name."

Barlasch broke off and thumped his brow with his fists, as if to awaken that dead memory. And all the while he was searching Désirée's face, with eyes made brighter and sharper than ever by starvation.

"And do you know what he came for—the Captain —for he never does anything in idleness He will run a great risk—but it is for a great purpose. Do you know what he came for?"

"No."

Barlasch jerked his head back and laughed.

"For you."

He turned and looked at her; but she had raised her clasped hands to her forehead, as if to shield her eyes from the light of the candle, and he could not see her face.

"Do you remember," said Barlasch, "that night when the patron was so angry—on the mat—when Mademoiselle Mathilde had to make her choice. It is your turn to-night. You have to make your choice. Will you go?"

"Yes," answered Désirée, behind her fingers.

"'If Mademoiselle will come,' he said to me, 'bring her to this place!' 'Yes, mon capitaine,' answered I. 'At any cost, Barlasch?' 'At any cost, mon capitaine.' And we are not men to break our words. I will take you there—at any cost, mademoiselle. And he will meet you there—at any cost."

And Barlasch expectorated emphatically into the fire, after the manner of low-born men.

"What a pity," he added reflectively, "that he is only an Englishman."

"When are we to go?" asked Désirée, still behind her barrier of clasped fingers.

"To-morrow night, after midnight. We have arranged it all—the Captain and I—at the outpost nearest to the river. He has influence. He has rendered services to the Russians, and the Russian commander will make a night attack on the outpost. In the confusion we get through. We arranged it together. He pays me well. It is a bargain, and I am to have my money. We shook hands on it, and those who saw us must have thought that I was buying fish. I, who have no money—and he, who had no fish."

CHAPTER XXX.

THE FULFILMENT.

And I have laboured somewhat in my time
And not been paid profusely

WHEN Désirée came down the next morning, she found Barlasch talking to himself and laughing as he prepared his breakfast.

He met her with a gay salutation, and seemed unable to control his hilarity.

"It is," he explained, "because to-night we shall be under fire. We shall be in danger. It makes me afraid, and I laugh. I cannot help it. When I am afraid, I laugh."

He bustled about the room, and Désirée saw that he had already opened his secret store beneath the floor, to take from it such delicacies as remained.

"You slept?" he asked sharply. "Yes, I can see you did. That is good, for to-night we shall be awake. And now you must eat."

For Barlasch was a materialist. He had fought death in one form or another all his life, and he knew that those who eat and sleep are better equipped for the battle than those who cherish high ideals or think great thoughts.

"It is a good thing," he said, looking at her, "that you are so slim. In a military coat—if you put on that short dress in which you skate, and your high boots—you will look like a soldier. It is a good thing that it is winter, for you can wear the hood of your military coat over your head, as they all do out in the trenches to keep their ears from falling. So you need not cut off your hair—all that golden hair. Name of thunder, that would be a pity, would it not?"

He turned to the fire and stirred his coffee reflectively.

"In my own country," he said, "a long time ago, there was a girl who had hair like yours. That is why we are friends, perhaps."

He gave a queer, short laugh, and took up his sheepskin coat preparatory to going out.

"I have my preparations to make," he said, with an air of importance. "There is much to be thought of. We had not long together, for the others were watching us. But we understand each other. I go now to give him the signal that it is for to-night. I have borrowed one of Lisa's dusters—a blue one that will show against the snow—with which to give him the signal. And he is watching from Zoppot with his telescope. That fat Lisa—if I had held up my finger, she would have fallen in love with me. It has always been so. These women——"

And he went away muttering.

If he had preparations to make, Désirée had no less.

She could take but little with her, and she was quitting the house which had always been her home so long as she could remember. Those trunks which Barlasch had so unhesitatingly recognized as coming from France were, it seemed, destined never to be used again. Mathilde had gone, taking with her her few simple possessions; for they had always been poor in the Frauengasse. Sebastian had departed on that journey which the traveller must face alone, taking naught with him. And it was characteristic of the man that he had left nothing behind him—no papers, no testament, no clue to that other life so different from his life in the Frauengasse that it must have lapsed into a fleeting, intangible memory, such as the brain is sometimes allowed to retain of a dream dreamt in this existence, or perhaps in another. Sebastian was gone—with his secret.

Désirée, alone with hers, was left in this quiet house for a few hours longer. Mechanically she set it in order. What would it matter to-morrow whether it were set in order or not? Who would come to note the last touches? She worked with that feverish haste which is responsible for much unnecessary woman's work in this world—the haste that owes its existence to the fear of having time to think. Many talk for the same reason. What a quiet world, if those who have nothing to say said nothing! But speech or work must fail at last, and lo! the thoughts are lying in wait.

Désirée's thoughts found their opportunity when she went into the drawing-room upstairs, where her wedding-breakfast had been set before the guests only eight months ago. The guests—De Casimir, the Gräfin, Sebastian, Mathilde, Charles!

Désirée stood alone now in the silent room. She did not look at the table. The guests were all gone. The dead past had buried its dead. She went to the window and drew aside the curtain as she had drawn it aside on her wedding-day to look down into the Frauengasse and see Louis d'Arragon. And again her heart leapt in her breast with that throb of fear. She turned where she stood, and looked at the door as if she expected to see Charles come in at it, laughing and gay, explaining (he was so good at explaining) his encounter in the street, and stepping aside to allow Louis to come forward. Louis, who looked at no one but her, and came into the room and into her life.

She had been afraid of him. She was afraid of him still. And her heart had leapt at the thought that he had been restlessly, sleeplessly thinking of her, working for her—had been to Vilna and back for her, and was now waiting for her beyond the barrier of Russian camp-fires. The dangers which made Barlasch laugh—and she knew they were real enough, for it was only a real danger that stirred something in the old soldier's blood to make him gay—these dangers were of no account. She knew, she had known instantly and for all time when she looked down into the Frauengasse and saw Louis, that nothing in heaven or earth could keep them apart.

She stood now, looking at the empty doorway. What was the rest of her life to be?

Barlasch returned in the afternoon. He was leisurely and inclined to contemplativeness. It would seem that his preparations having all been completed, he was left with nothing to do. War is a purifier; it clears the social atmosphere and puts womanly men and manly women into their right places. It is also a simplifier; it teaches us to know how little we really require in daily life, and how many of the environments with which men and women hamper themselves are superfluous and the fruit of idleness.

"I have nothing to do," said Barlasch, "I will cook a careful dinner. All that I have saved in money I cannot carry away; all that was stored beneath the floor must be left there. It is often so in war."

He had told Désirée that they would have to walk

twelve miles across the snow-clad marshes bordering the frozen Vistula, between midnight and dawn. It needed no telling that they could carry little with them.

"You will have to make a new beginning in life," he said curtly, "with the clothes upon your back. How many times have I done it—the Saints alone know! But take money, if you have it in gold or silver. Mine is all in copper groschen, and it is too heavy to carry. I have never yet been anywhere that money was not useful—and name of a dog! I have never had it."

So Désirée divided what money she possessed with Barlasch, who added it carefully up and repeated several times for accuracy the tale of what he had received. For, like many who do not hesitate to steal, he was very particular in money matters.

"As for me," he said, "I shall make a new beginning, too. The Captain will enable me to get back to France, when I shall go to the Emperor again. It is no place for one of the Old Guard, here with Rapp. I am getting old, but he will find something for me to do, that little Emperor."

At midnight they set out, quitting the house in the Frauengasse noiselessly. The street was quiet enough, for half the houses were empty now. Their footsteps were inaudible on the trodden snow. It was a dark night and not cold; for the great frosts of this terible winter were nearly over.

Barlasch carried his musket and bayonet. He had instructed Désirée to walk in front of him, should they meet a patrol. But Rapp had no men to spare for patrolling the town. There was no spirit left in Dantzig; for typhus and starvation patrolled the narrow streets.

They quitted the town to the north-west, near the Oliva Gate. There was no guard-house here because Langfuhr was held by the French, and Rapp's outposts were three miles out on the road to Zoppot.

"I have played this game for fifty years," said Barlasch, with a low laugh, when they reached the earthworks, completed, at such enormous cost of life and strength, by Rapp; "follow me and do as I do. When I stoop, stoop; when I crawl, crawl; when I run, run."

For he was a soldier now and nothing else. He stood erect, and looked round him with the air of a young man — ready, keen, alert. Then he moved forward with confidence towards the high land which terminates in the Johannesberg, where the peaceful Dantzigers now repair on a Sunday afternoon to drink thin beer and admire the view.

Below them on the right hand lay the marshes, a white expanse of snow with a single dark line drawn across it—the Langfuhr road with its double border of trees.

Barlasch turned once or twice to make sure that Désirée was following him; but he added nothing to his brief instructions. When he gained the summit of the tableland which runs parallel with the coast and the Langfuhr road, he paused for breath.

"When I crawl, crawl. When I run, run," he whispered again; and led the way. He went up the bed of a stream, turning his back to the coast, and at a certain point stopped and by a gesture of the hand bade Désirée crouch down and wait till he returned. He came back and signed to her to quit the bed of the stream and follow him. When she came up to the tableland, she found that they were quite close to a camp-fire. Through the low pines she could perceive the dark outline of a house.

"Now run," whispered Barlasch, leading the way across an open space which seemed to extend to the line of the horizon. Without looking back, Désirée ran—her only thought was a sudden surprise that Barlasch could move so quickly and silently.

When he gained the shelter of some trees, he threw himself down on the snow, and Désirée coming up to him found him breathlessly holding his sides and laughing aloud.

"We are through the lines," he gasped, "name of a dog, I was so frightened. There they go—pam! pam! Buz . z . . z . ."

And he imitated the singing buzz of the bullets humming through the trees over their heads. For half a dozen shots were fired, while he was yet speaking, from behind the camp-fires. There were no more, however, and presently, having recovered his breath, Barlasch rose.

"Come," he said, "we have a long walk. *En route.*"

They made a great circuit in the pine-woods, through which Barlasch led the way with an unerring skill, and descending towards the plain far beyond Langfuhr they came out on to a lower tableland, below which the great marshes of the Vistula stretched in the darkness, slowly merging at last into the sea.

"Those," said Barlasch, pausing at the edge of the slope, "those are the lights of Oliva, where the Russians are. That line of lights straight in front is the Russian fleet lying off Zoppot, and with them are English ships. One of them is the little ship of Captain d'Arragon. And he will take you home with him; for the ship is ordered to England, to Plymouth—which is across the Channel from my own country. Ah—cristi! I sometimes want to see my own country again — and my own people — mademoiselle."

He went on a few paces and then stopped again, and in the darkness held up one hand, commanding silence. It was the churches of Dantzig striking the hour.

"Six o'clock," he whispered, "it will soon be dawn. Yes—we are half an hour too early."

He sat down, and, by a gesture, bade Désirée sit beside him.

"Yes," he said, "the Captain told me that he is bound for England to convoy larger ships, and you will sail in one of them. He has a home in the west of England, and he will take you there—a sister or a mother, I forget which—some woman. You cannot get on without women—you others. It is there that you will be happy, as the bon Dieu meant you to be. It is only in England that no one fears Napoleon. One may have a husband there and not fear that he will be killed. One may have children and not tremble for them— and it is that that makes you happy—you women."

Presently he rose and led the way down the slope. At the foot of it, he paused, and, pointing out a long line of trees, said in a whisper—

"He is there—where there are three taller trees. Between us and those trees are the French outposts. At dawn the Russians attack the outposts, and during the attack we have simply to go through it to those trees. There is no other way—that is the rendezvous. Those three tall trees. When I give the word, you get up and run to those trees—run without pausing, without looking round. I will follow. It is you he has come for—not Barlasch. You think I know nothing Bah! I know everything. I have always known it—your poor little secret."

They lay on the snow crouching in a ditch until a grey line appeared low down in the Eastern sky and the horizon slowly distinguished itself from the thin thread of cloud that nearly always awaits the rising of the sun in Northern latitudes.

A minute later the dark group of trees broke into intermittent flame and the sharp, short "Hurrah!" of the Cossacks, like an angry bark, came sweeping across the plain on the morning breeze.

"Not yet," whispered Barlasch, with a gay chuckle of enjoyment. "Not yet—not yet. Listen, the bullets are not coming here, but are going past to the right of us. When you go, keep to the left. Slowly at first— keep a little breath till the end. Now, up! Mademoiselle, run; name of thunder, let us run!"

Désirée did not understand which were the French lines and which the line of Russian attack. But there was a clear way to the three trees which stood above the rest, and she went towards them. She knew she could not run so far, so she walked. Then the bullets, instead of passing to the right, seemed to play round her—like bees in a garden on a summer day—and she ran until she was tired.

The trees were quite close now, and the sky was light behind them. Then she saw Louis coming towards her, and she ran into his arms. The sound of the humming bullets was still in her dazed brain, and she touched him all over with her gloved hand as she clung to him, as a mother touches her child when it has fallen, to see whether it be hurt.

"How was I to know?" she whispered breathlessly. "How was I to know that you were to come into my life?"

The bullets did not matter, it seemed, nor the roar of the firing to the right of them. Nothing mattered—except that Louis must know that she had never loved Charles.

He held her and said nothing. And she wanted him to say nothing. Then she remembered Barlasch, and looked back over her shoulder.

"Where is Barlasch?" she asked, with a sudden sinking at her heart.

"He is coming slowly," replied Louis. "He came slowly behind you all the time, so as to draw the fire away from you."

They turned and waited for Barlasch, who seemed to be going in the wrong direction with an odd vagueness in his movements. Louis ran towards him with Désirée at his heels.

"Ça-y-est," said Barlasch; which cannot be translated, and yet has many meanings. "Ça-y-est."

And he sat down slowly on the snow. He sat quite upright and rigid, and in the cold light of the

Baltic dawn they saw the meaning of his words. One hand was within his fur coat. He drew it out, and concealed it from Désirée behind his back. He did not seem to see them, but presently he put out his hand and lightly touched Désirée. Then he turned to Louis with that confidential drop of the voice with which he always distinguished his friends from those who were not his friends.

"What is she doing?" he asked. "I cannot see in the dark. Is it not dark? I thought it was. What is she doing? Saying a prayer? What—because I have my affair? Hey, mademoiselle. You may leave it to me. I will get in, I tell you that."

He put his finger to his nose, and then shook it from side to side with an air of deep cunning.

"Leave it to me. I shall slip in. Who will stop an old man, who has many wounds? Not St. Peter, assuredly. Let him try. And if the good God hears a commotion at the gate, He will only shrug His shoulders. He will say to St. Peter, 'Let pass; it is only Papa Barlasch!'"

And then there was silence. For Barlasch had gone to his own people.

THE END.

BIBLIOLIFE

Old Books Deserve a New Life
www.bibliolife.com

Did you know that you can get most of our titles in our trademark **EasyScript**™ print format? **EasyScript**™ provides readers with a larger than average typeface, for a reading experience that's easier on the eyes.

Did you know that we have an ever-growing collection of books in many languages?

Order online:
www.bibliolife.com/store

Or to exclusively browse our **EasyScript**™ collection:
www.bibliogrande.com

At BiblioLife, we aim to make knowledge more accessible by making thousands of titles available to you – quickly and affordably.

Contact us:
BiblioLife
PO Box 21206
Charleston, SC 29413

Printed in Great Britain by
Amazon.co.uk, Ltd.,
Marston Gate.